THE YALE CHRONICLES
OF AMERICA SERIES

The
Cotton
Kingdom

A Chronicle
of the
Old South

by
William E. Dodd

1978

Toronto
Glasgow, Brook & Co.

New York
United States Publishers
Association, Inc.

CONTENTS

THE COTTON KINGDOM

∴

CHAPTER I

THE region which in the middle of the last century was known as the Cotton Kingdom extended a distance of more than a thousand miles from South Carolina to the neighborhood of San Antonio, Texas. The breadth of this country, from north to south, ranged from two hundred miles in Carolina and Texas to six or seven hundred miles in the Mississippi Valley. The land on which cotton could be easily grown measured perhaps as much as four hundred thousand square miles in 1850, if we count Texas, Arkansas, and Florida, which were then, however, yielding only small crops. Large areas in the lower South were not suited to cotton culture, although they contributed to the cotton kingdom other economic resources of no small value. The pine barrens of South Carolina, Georgia, Alabama, Mississippi, and Louisiana could produce immense quantities of lumber; and the hills and mountains of the two Carolinas, Georgia, and Alabama supplied a large portion of the grain and the whisky consumed on the plantations.

The cotton belt is a well-watered country with an annual rainfall almost twice as great as that of Illinois or New York. Moreover the snows of the lower Appalachians which lie upon the densely wooded highlands and towering mountains during half the year are carried off through the eastern half of the cotton country by numerous rivers whose average volume is as great as that of the Susquehanna or the Ohio. In addition to these large streams of water there are thousands of smaller rivers, rising among the hills and struggling through the marshes of the low country, which enrich the land and furnish unsurpassed facilities for transportation. In lower South Carolina and Georgia the network of navigable waters brings every parish into touch with Charleston or other coast towns. Farther west the Chattahoochee, the Tombigbee, the Yazoo, the Mississippi itself, the Red, the Sabine, the Trinity, the Brazos, and the Colorado form systems of communication

which make it easy to market all sorts of crops —
particularly cotton, which can be hauled profitably a hundred miles to the river wharves. It is
thus a fact of great importance in the study of
the lower South that the larger part of the cotton
region, somewhat like the tobacco region of colonial times, is within easy reach of Atlantic or
Gulf ports.

The soil of the cotton belt, though not so fertile
as that of the upper Mississippi valley, was ex-
ceedingly productive. In South Carolina and
Georgia it had a reddish hue like that of the Virginia up-country; in Alabama and Mississippi it
was dark like that of the prairie region of the
Middle West; and everywhere it was soft and easily
tillable. It produced corn as readily as cotton, but
wheat did not thrive on so loose and open a soil.
The seasons were so long that two or often three
crops of vegetables were raised in a year, with
the warm sun and abundant rains as the benevo-
lent allies of the farmer. Peas, potatoes, beans,
and fruit could be grown so quickly and abun-
dantly that the problem of subsistence during the
Civil War, for example, was much simpler than
in any of the European countries fighting in the
First World War.

But before the cotton-planters overran the country during the two decades preceding the beginning of this story, this area was virgin country and, with the exception of certain prairie districts, was covered with dense forests, while its river-bottoms were still tangled, impenetrable swamps. And even as late as 1860 the clearing of new lands was a large part of the planter's work. This was done by cutting away the brambles and dense undergrowth and then "deadening" the larger trees by a process of belting or taking away the bark near the ground and thus preventing further growth. This clearing of the forests let the sunlight fall upon the soil and enabled the planter to produce his first crop at a minimum of expense. But the tall, dead trees, from which the winds tore off branches and strewed them over the ground, gave the countryside a somber, despoiled appearance, and seemed the skeletons of the monarchs of the forest crying aloud against the desecration of nature and the sheer waste of the finest timber in the world.

The immediate profits of cotton-growing were so much more easily realized than the remote rewards of conservation that the spoliation of timber-lands continued with a ruthlessness unparalleled elsewhere in the world. Men became hardened to this work until the felling of trees became a pastime; and when there was nothing else for slaves to do, they were sent to the "new grounds" to cut timber and burn logs with the idea that older land would soon need to be abandoned and the new be added to the arable fields. West of South Carolina the land was bought at government sales at a dollar and a quarter an acre or was even seized without the formality of a purchase by squatters who entered the public domain, built their cabins, cleared patches of land, and then defied the Federal officials to oust them. The ease with which one might raise a crop of cotton and the relatively large returns which it brought drew men of all classes to the lower South. Thousands of square miles of rich lands within easy distance of navigable rivers gave the people of the region a sense of new opportunity, a feeling that the world belongs to him who can exploit it, and a restless craving for a new life and wide acres — all of which influenced profoundly not only the lower South but the whole course of American history. Between 1820 and 1850 almost anything seemed possible to the enterprising man of the cotton country.

Until 1830 Indian tribes held immense tracts in

Georgia, Alabama, and Mississippi. The Chero-
kees, the Creeks, the Choctaws, and the Chicka-
saws counted many thousand warriors; they dwelt
upon good cotton lands and, what was worse, they
had been taught many of the arts of civilization by
the Federal Government and had been encouraged
to become orderly citizens of the United States.
This policy tended to make of the Indian a per-
manent holder of his land; and in many, many
instances these "wards of the nation" had become
owners of good homes, masters of slaves, and successful cotton-planters.

The planters of Georgia first, and later those of
the other States who coveted these lands with a
covetousness unimagined by the kingly exploiter of
Naboth's vineyard in ancient times, vowed that
the Indians should not be allowed to develop
settled, civilized communities. Since the planters
were represented in Congress and the natives had
recourse only to executive protection, the contest
was most unequal; and, when President Jackson
gave the Indians over to the tender mercies of their
enemies, there was no help for them. The planters
had their way, and the Indian lands were rapidly
converted into cotton plantations. Pretty cot-
tages and squalid wigwams, fertile fields and wild

hunting-grounds, negro slaves, horses, and farming implements all had to be sacrificed without any other reparation than doles of money and such lands as the Indian could settle beyond the Red River.

Having secured the vast area of land, the planters had then to obtain the labor requisite to cultivate their new acres. Between the close of the second war with England and the annexation of Texas this problem solved itself. On the river-bottoms of Maryland, Virginia, and North Carolina, or in the counties which bordered on the piedmont region of those States, there were more than a million slaves whose numbers doubled every twenty years. Since the demand for tobacco had not greatly increased since 1800, there was no profitable employment for these growing hordes of blacks. The owner of slaves in this region could not move to the up-country west of the Blue Ridge, for there were no roads or canals by which to transport the wheat and corn which would be his chief crops in the new country. If he went still farther west to Kentucky or Missouri, he found tobacco-growing already well past the stage of profitable employment of slaves. There were left the wide prairies of Indiana and Illinois, but as the laws of those States did not recognize slavery the well-to-do Southerner could not go there except at the sacrifice of the larger part of his property.

The slaveholder of the older South might emigrate to the lower South, taking his negroes with him, or he might sell his servants and eke out a living for himself and his family on the old homestead. It was a hard choice, but it could not well be avoided. Thousands emigrated and added their numbers and wealth to the cotton belt; other thousands sold their slaves and thus added to the increasing volume of labor needed to clear the forests and grow the cotton crops of the lower South. Year after year masters and slaves found their way to the new economic El Dorado, and year after year the influence and power of the planters became more evident to the rest of the country.

In the tobacco country or among the foothills of the older South another and larger class of people found that society was fast hardening around them and was compelling them to take subordinate social stations. They likewise emigrated, and many, very many, of them went to the Northwest, where they "took up" lands and raised just enough grain and pork to sustain their families.

Even more of them went to Alabama and Mississippi, where they obtained a small tract of land, bought a negro with their first crop of cotton, and set up as planters "on the make." These pioneers became the most resolute and uncompromising of all the enemies of the Indians and the most ardent advocates of the institution of slavery.

Thus practically the whole increase of the slave and the white population in the older South was emigrating and most of it was going to the new cotton region. In some counties of the seaboard States, such as Virginia, the population decreased by half in one or two decades, and everywhere the lands and houses of well-to-do people declined in value. Jefferson's magnificent home sold in 1829 for about $3000; Madison struggled manfully but in vain to avoid disposing of his family servants; and John Randolph talked about running away from his plantation to avoid bankruptcy. What was the reason for this state of affairs?

Old Virginia and her neighbors were caught between the upper and the nether economic millstones. Disavow it as they would, their most profitable product was the slave who could be sold. Negroes alone increased in value. It is no wonder that statesmen of the older South saw in this traffic a means of rehabilitating their declining commonwealths.[1]

The census of 1850 gives the lower South, including Arkansas, 2,137,000 white people and 1,841,000 blacks, nearly all of whom were slaves — a total population of nearly 4,000,000. The great majority of whites lived in counties where slavery had little influence; and nearly all the slaves lived in the cotton belt, that is, in the districts within easy reach of the rivers. The upbuilding of this region had been accomplished almost entirely within thirty years, and the period of rapid growth and change had now come to a close.

Practically all the produce of these lower Southern States was exported. Their cotton sold in 1850 for $102,000,000; their sugar, for $14,800,000; and their rice, for $2,600,000 — a total of $119,-400,000. The exports of the whole country were only $203,000,000 in 1850, but while the larger part of these exports thus originated in the cotton States, less than a fourth of all the imports came through Southern ports. Charleston, for example, exported from $8,000,000 to $10,000,000 worth of goods

[1] The lure of the lower South drew also from Boston, New York, Philadelphia, and Pittsburgh, enterprising and ambitious young men, like Sergeant Prentiss and John A. Quitman, who in a few years became great planters and influential public leaders.

each year, but imported scarcely over $2,000,000.
The balance of trade was also against Mobile and
other Southern cities. But because nearly half the
people of the cotton States were property, the per
capita wealth of the planter was much greater
than that of the Easterner; and, notwithstanding
the most unfavorable balance of trade against his
section, he made great display of his wealth.

Rapidly increasing wealth makes one hunger the
more for still greater wealth and a wider area for
one's operations. Even before the Indians had all
moved across the Mississippi, the planters began
a most vigorous campaign for the annexation
of Texas. From New Orleans, Vicksburg, and
Natchez, from Mobile and Montgomery, even from
Charleston and Savannah, adventurous men and
prospective planters hurried into the disputed
region, took up lands, and began the cultivation
of cotton and the importation of slaves from the
older South. They were winning for the United
States a new and promising empire. With equal
zest and enthusiasm men from Tennessee, Kentucky, and Missouri hastened to join their Southern brethren and to help them wrest the coveted
province from the hand of Mexico. The Revolution of 1836 brought independence to the Republic

of Texas and eventually annexation to the American Union, through a coalition of Southern and Western party groups. The Mexican War followed, and still other vast areas of land were annexed to the United States. What cotton-planters wanted, Congress somehow found a way to grant.

Nor was the case wholly different in the greater matter of the national tariff. When, in 1828, the South and the West united to place Jackson in the President's chair, it was definitely understood that the "tariff of abominations" was to be abolished or greatly reduced. The exigencies of national politics caused Jackson to falter and delay. South Carolina allowed the new President four years to make up his mind. When he was still uncertain in 1832, that State proceeded to nullify the offensive national statute; the President then threatened war; South Carolina thereupon paused; but the outcome was the definite abandonment of the higher tariff policy in favor of the lower rates of the compromise tariff of 1833. Every South Carolinian thought that the planters had once again had their way; and South Carolinians were scattered over all the cotton States.

If ever people were taught to believe themselves invincible in politics, it was the people of the cotton

country during the two decades which preceded
1850. A vast region of rich cotton lands had been
rapidly opened up to them; the natives had been
driven beyond the distant Red River; a new State
embracing more than two hundred and fifty thousand square miles had been annexed; and the
protective tariff policy by which Eastern manu-
facturers sought to possess the American markets
free from competition had been abandoned. Why
then might not the gentleman of the lower South
boast of his growing riches and of his control of
national affairs?

The lower South had been and still was an
outwardly irreligious, dram-drinking, and dueling
section. The French priests had built a compact
religious community in and about New Orleans,
but they had not pushed this work up the rivers
and out into the great stretches of country where
plantation life was dominant. Nor was their easy-
going moral system entirely adapted to the needs
of rural life. The cathedral church, the monastery,
and the parochial schools filled the round of the
priest's life and duties. The saving of souls in
distant plantations was not his especial concern.
Dueling and card-playing and horse-racing were

not beyond the range of his own interests; why should he stir up a crusade against them? The faith of the Roman Catholic Church was, therefore, comparatively stagnant in the lower South. Aside from a few churches in Louisiana and Charleston, firmly established parishes in Mobile, and a diocese in Florida, this branch of the Christian Church had not become a force in the planter civilization.

If the founders of the Roman Catholic Church in the lower South were content to let the planters go their own way and to confine their activities to the larger towns, the builders of the Church of England were no more enterprising. They established their churches in Charleston, Savannah, and other towns, and set up chapels of ease in the outlying parishes — half-way houses, as it were, to the true church in the city — but they were not consumed with zeal to save the lost souls of the hordes of men who filled up the back country. Gambling and horse-racing and card-playing were to the Anglican clergy what they were to the Catholic priests, a means of hastening weary hours away. Even dueling among vestrymen of high standing was not to them one of the crimes to be denounced from the pulpit. They condoned slavery at first and later proclaimed it God's way of saving the

souls of the heathen. Good sermons were indeed
read on Sabbath days in the churches of Charleston and the other cities, and many charities occupied the attention of the Episcopalians of the
lower South; but these gentle ministrations did
not affect the red-blooded men and women who
were building in the open country the foundations
of a great section of the American Union.

Men of the cotton country might live freely,
might partake of the joys of this world, and might
even deny the fundamentals of the Christian faith
without feeling that everlasting penance must be
done in the world to come. Nor was there great
religious or social scruple if aristocratic blood ran
in negro veins or if fine young gentlemen kept half-
breed mistresses. Only one must not bring one's
hybrid offspring to Mardi Gras or seat them with
the family in the cathedral church in New Orleans or St. Michael's in Charleston. Men drank
the best and oldest wines of France till they were
wholly drunk; they built the best of theaters and
engaged troupes of actors from England whose repu-
tations for immorality would have scandalized all
New England; they even lured assemblies of clergymen to witness their races and take chances on
their steeds. There was thus an un-Puritan and

continental sort of life in the older communities
of the young cotton kingdom which was in time
wholly to disappear.

Another vanishing social group consisted of the
high English gentry whose grandfathers had been
received at the Court of St. James in the days of
the Georges or who had chased the famous Black-
beard or who had even turned sea-robbers themselves. They, too, had made their fortunes in the
unsettled eighteenth century; but in the decades
which preceded 1850 they were fast disappearing
from among the increasing numbers of cotton-
planters. They had spread themselves over the
lands of South Carolina, built their houses far in-
land, and mingled their blood with people of less
aristocratic mold. The Pinckneys, the Rhetts,
and the Petigrus were merged into the new aristocracy of the country, although they still owned
houses in Charleston, held pews in the oldest
churches, and made a fetish of their St. Cecilia
Society, into whose sacred precincts unhallowed
feet seldom dared to tread. By the middle of the
century it was not so much the State of South
Carolina that drew out the loyalty and devotion
of the planter aristocracy; the building of a new
economic and social order based on an enlarged

planter group occupied men's thoughts and purposes in much the same way that the spread of
Kultur was to be the mission of the Pan Germans
of a latter day. South Carolina contributed
most to the making of that lower South which was
to dominate so large a part of the national thought
in the two decades before the Civil War.

An important racial element was contributed to
the life of South Carolina by the French Huguenots of high intellectual endowment and even literary culture whose ancestors had driven in family
coaches and had read good books for three genera-
tions. Unsurpassed in commercial pursuits, they
heaped up fortunes which made their names
known on both sides of the Atlantic during the
Revolution and the decades which followed the
adoption of the Federal Constitution. But aristocratic groups seldom maintain themselves. The
Huguenots were fast merging into the planter-
lawyer class, and when cotton became king in the
South, their quaint accent was about all that remained to mark them as a race apart.

In New Orleans were old French families dating
back to the days of the *Grand Monarque* himself,
who had houses on St. Charles, Royal, or Toulouse
street, owned plantations on the river or offices

on Canal Street, and attended French opera in the
evening. Their wealth was invested in slaves or
sugar or cotton; their quaint old coaches were seen
along the Strand or the Esplanade; and their children took dancing lessons with French masters
who showed both young and old what was good
form in France.

So many Spaniards had come into the colony
during the Spanish rule and so many English roy-
alists from Revolutionary America that society
was wonderfully mixed in New Orleans. All
nationalities, including Germans and Italians,
entered into the life of the lower Mississippi. And
there were many creoles with the blood of several
races in their veins. Octoroons and half-breeds
and pure blacks made up the free negro population,
which had a life of its own unlike that in any other
city in the country. Some negroes were gentlemen
with a standing amongst other gentlemen which
would scandalize Southerners of a later day. In
New Orleans as in Charleston, there were negro
owners of slaves who played a considerable part
in the civic life, were among the stanchest defenders of slavery as an institution, and were
bitterly opposed to all who talked of setting free
their slaves.

Outwardly New Orleans was the most European of all American cities in 1850, and its music, literature, and manners were European quite as much as American. But the tone was changing. Hillhouse and Story, Slocomb and Eustis, were names of families that did not remind one of either France or Spain. And there were many street names that bespoke the influence of the Yankees who had long ruled the city with a strange lack of reverence for old things and old times. New Orleans was definitely passing from the epoch of Catholic and fur-trading supremacy to that of Protestantism and cotton. Dr. Clapp, the great Boston preacher, and General Gaines, the hero of many battles, were the visible evidences of a new era; yet it must be recognized that French influence contributed much that was valuable to the plantation system.

The hills of North Carolina, Virginia, and Tennessee reared thousands and tens of thousands of plain, poor folk who made the bone and sinew of the lower South. They knew nothing of the gentle ways of Charleston or of the French manners of New Orleans. They built their cabins all over the up-country from what is now Charlotte to Atlanta; they overran northern Alabama and the Tombigbee Valley; and they "took up" lands in Mississippi and Louisiana. It was they who made by far the larger part of the new country. While the older Virginians brought with them their slaves and their good middle-class manners, and while the gentry of Charleston and New Orleans boasted of their families and their culture, these people adhered firmly to their stern Presbyterian faith or to the warmer religious emotionalism of the Baptists and Methodists.

To be sure, many of these settlers from the poorer districts of the older South were not saints or of the stuff of which saints are made, but there were enough of the earnest and devout to make the salt for the saving of the whole social lump. Slowly these elements were merged with the older order, learned somewhat of the elegance and form which made the Carolina and Louisiana stocks so attractive, and contributed the largest element to the new society which the world always associates with cotton and slavery.

For the moment a good deal of the religious inheritance from Jonathan Edwards, Whitefield, and Wesley, which the "new light" preachers had delivered to the poorer white people of the South, was lost in the migration to the cotton country. The frontier has always been indifferent to formal

religion. The free life of the forest, the conflict
with the Indians, and the struggle with nature
tended to make men forget the catechism and
the hymnal. Nor did the easy-going manners of
the older planters, the horses, the hounds, and the
illicit loves with squaws and negro women, stiffen
the backbone of personal morality. An affair of
honor, a duel which always followed the slightest
insult among men of family, was attractive to men
who were just climbing to the higher rungs of the
social ladder; and where law and social solidarity
developed slowly these newer men quickly learned
to defend themselves, to be the avengers of their
own and their family's wrongs. Every man carried
his weapon in his pocket and he was not slow to use
it. Public gatherings were not the safest places for
men of hot tempers.

And where the weather at all seasons was open,
court days, barbecues, and even religious gatherings, not infrequently were the scenes of encounters
between gentlemen and of fisticuffs between men
of lower degree. Feuds and lawsuits were en-
gendered and prolonged to the great satisfaction of
lawyers and hangers-on of the courts. To these
occasions of legal conflict were added the myriad
suits about land titles and preëmption claims which

gave sustenance to a host of attorneys. Where money came easily it went easily. Sergeant Prentiss, a New England lawyer-orator of the first importance in the cotton kingdom, received a fee of $50,000 for the conduct of a single case in the Supreme Court of Mississippi; and Reuben Davis became a state-wide hero in the defense of an acknowledged murderer.

As one reviews these elements and forces that entered into the make-up of the lower South in 1850, it becomes plain that this was a region of immense potentiality. Its great waterfalls might run the wheels of many thousand industrial plants, if Southerners ever turned their minds in the direction of manufacturing. Its fertile lands might feed cattle enough to supply the whole national demand for meat. Its harbors were ample for large fleets of ocean-going vessels. The people who had rushed in, dispossessed the native Indians, cleared the lands, became planters, established commonwealths, and sent spokesmen to Congress, were native Americans, with rare exceptions. They were tobacco farmers from the older South, poor whites from all the Atlantic States, Carolina gentlemen, French settlers in Louisiana,

and Scotch-Irish farmers from the mountain districts of Pennsylvania, Maryland, and Virginia.
The German element, which had formed so large
a part of the Southern population at the time of
the Revolution, could be detected only in proper
names here and there and in an occasional *Verein*.
Their language, manners, and religion had nearly
everywhere given way to the dominant Anglo-
Saxon civilization.   The lower South was a region
of vast opportunity but of wavering democratic
faith; it was a region of American traditions, except
in its growing devotion to slavery.   If its political
and social leaders should succeed in uniting all its
groups, in moderating its growing ambitions, and
in educating its great mass of illiterate people, it
must of necessity become one of the greatest sections of the United States and dictate to a large
extent the course of national history.   Would these
conditions be adequately met?   Was it possible for
the planters to develop the wisest counsels?

CHAPTER II

THE amalgamation of the various elements and forces of the population which composed the cotton States in 1850 was strikingly paralleled by the rapid concentration of economic power in three or four thousand families who lived on the best lands and received three-fourths of the returns from the yearly exports. Two-thirds of the white people of the South had no connection with slavery and received only a very small part of the returns of the community output. A thousand families received over $50,000,000 a year, while all the remaining 666,000 families received only about $60,000,000. While these figures do not show such extreme concentration of wealth in a few hands as the facts of our own day disclose, they do nevertheless reveal a dangerous tendency.

Though there was some discontent even in the South at this menace of concentrated wealth, no effort was made to limit the size of men's fortunes.

The tendency was to divide the great numbers of slaves owned by one master into plantation groups of something like a hundred each. A thousand acres of land and a hundred slaves made a unit which was regarded as the most productive; but one man might own ten such units and never be made to bear inheritance or super-taxes. The Hairstons owned as many as 1700 slaves distributed over plantations in Virginia, Alabama, and Mississippi; Howell Cobb of Georgia was pointed out as the master of a thousand negroes; while the Aikens of South Carolina and Joseph Davis (brother of Jefferson Davis) of Mississippi were counted as millionaires.

There was something factitious about the growing wealth of the great masters. The number of slaves owned was believed to be an index of wealth. The greater the number of slaves one owned, the greater one's riches; and the number of slaves increased rapidly, even in the cotton belt. As fortune would have it, the price of cotton tended to rise during the period of 1845 to 1860. This rise in prices added a hundred per cent to the value of land, and it also added nearly a hundred per cent to the value of each slave. A cotton-planter had only to be a kind master and a reasonably good

manager, or employ good overseers, and he could
not avoid the rapid accumulation of wealth. He
simply grew rich.

The rising price of cotton naturally increased
the output of the plantations and gave the owners
of slaves a sense of security which they had not
known in the older South for fifty years. Between 1850 and 1860 the annual cotton crop increased from 2,500,000 to 5,000,000 bales, and thus
more than doubled the wealth of the planters.
What exaggerated the situation was the fact that
these huge crops did not meet the demands of
European and New England mills. Thus every
way one turned, the fortunes of the cotton-growers
increased and the difficulties of regulating or limit-
ing the evil of slavery increased. Here seems to be
an illustration of the saying that prosperity is
quite as unfortunate in its effects as poverty.

Every year added to the wealth of him who had
and seemed to take away from him who had not.
A healthy negro man was worth in 1845 about
$750; in 1860 the same slave, although fifteen years
older, was worth in the market a third more, and a
young negro man or woman readily sold for $1500. [1]

[1] New Orleans *Picayune*, August 8, 1858: "Seven slaves were sold
by the sheriff yesterday, without guarantee, at an average of $1,538."

There was no help for it. Economic laws concentrated the wealth of the South in the cotton region. Owners of slaves, as we have already seen, did not like to sell their servants, but they did sell them under these circumstances, and there was a constant stream of unwilling slave emigration from the tobacco country to the lower South. Cotton proved to be the irresistible magnet. It was doubtless these conditions which moved Lincoln to make his remarkable statement of 1854 that he did not know what to do about slavery: "I surely will not blame them for not doing what I should not know how to do myself. If all earthly power were given me, I should not know what to do as to the existing institution."[1]

But while the great planters were undoubtedly absorbing a disproportionate part of the wealth of the South, and while economic conditions were daily making more difficult the problem of the statesman who really loved the country, much if not most of this outward wealth found its way out of the cotton region. Leading Southern towns exported annually three or four times as much as they imported. New York, on the other hand, imported twice as much as she exported. Each year

[1] The Peoria Speech of October 4, 1854.

$100,000,000 worth of foreign goods came into the United States through her custom-house, while only $50,000,000 worth went out that way. The same thing was true of Philadelphia and Boston. The cotton-planters, with their wide-spread fields and their troops of negro laborers, were buying the bulk of their goods in the North and selling the whole of their output either to Europe or to the North at prices fixed in the world market. The merchants of New York, Boston, and Philadelphia thus reaped enormous profits.

In the realm of finance and banking there was a still stronger limitation upon the concentration of the profits of the cotton industry in the lower South. Men were chiefly interested in supplying their daily necessities from their own plantations, and the only commercial goods which they used were purchased from the North. As a result the planters paid little attention to matters of banking and credit. Although New Orleans was one of the greatest exporting cities in the country, the amount of money on deposit in her banks was insignificant. Less than a third of the returns on the cotton which annually left her docks ever found place in her financial institutions. On the other hand, New York or Philadelphia always had on deposit more money than the total value of her exports. What was true of New Orleans was true of the cotton belt as a whole. Though the cotton, rice, and sugar of the South sold for $119,400,000 in 1850, the total bank deposits of the region amounted to only some $20,000,000. Ten years later, when the value of the crops had increased to more than $200,000,000, less than $30,000,000 were deposited in the banks of the cotton and sugar belt.

Nor was it different in the matter of loans or specie or banking capital. While agricultural production was concentrated in the comparatively small area where cotton could be grown and the returns all seemed to be going to the planters, the evidence is conclusive that far the greater part of the proceeds was left in the hands of those who supplied the South with its necessaries and its luxuries. The earnings of the slave plantations were thus consumed by tariffs, freights, commissions, and profits which the Southerners had to pay. Southern towns were only marts of trade, not depositories of the crops of surrounding or distant areas. Thus while the planters monopolized the cotton industry, drew to themselves the surplus of slaves, and apparently increased their wealth enormously, they were really but custodians of these returns, administrators of the wealth of Northern men who really ultimately received the profits of Southern plantations and Southern slavery.

If some planters saw this dangerous tendency and sought frantically to check it, the majority of men were oblivious of it and endeavored to emulate the delusive riches of the great planters. The small farmer, the tenant, and the piney-woods squatter, so well described by Frederick Law Olmsted,[1] all contributed to the power and prestige of the industrial leaders. They produced but little surplus — a bale of cotton, a little fresh beef or pork, poultry, and eggs. This produce they carried on ox-carts or rickety wagons drawn by poverty-stricken horses to the nearest plantation towns and bought in exchange a New England bonnet for the wife, New England shoes for the husband and sons, or a little coffee or molasses for the family table. Although these people rarely became members of the privileged order,[2] they were closely bound to it, tributary in their small way to the great planter aristocracy.

[1] Olmsted, Frederick Law, *A Journey in the Seaboard Slave States*, New York, 1856; *A Journey in the Back Country*, New York, 1860.

[2] Hiram G. Runnels of Mississippi, who rose to be Governor in 1836, belonged to this class.

Another class of Southerners contributed in similar manner to the master group. They were the so-called "crackers" or "hill-billies" of northern Georgia and north-central Alabama, and the poorer whites who dwelt on the semibarren lands which the planters refused to cultivate or had worn out by their reckless methods of cultivation. They sometimes owned a few slaves, made a score of bales of cotton, and raised some wheat and corn for the planter market. Their net returns amounted to $100 or $200 per year and their homes bore a somewhat better aspect than did the cabins of the piney-woods people. The great majority of Southern whites belonged to these classes. They lived on the poorer lands in the cotton belt — on the hills that border the lower reaches of the Appalachian Mountains or on the sandy ridges of Louisiana and Texas. They were the inarticulate masses. Sometimes, as in the case of Andrew Johnson, twice Governor of Tennessee, or Joseph E. Brown of Georgia, the inveterate enemy of Jefferson Davis during the Civil War, they might rise to power and influence, but the great masses of them could hardly hope to see better days.

Like the piney-woods men, the farmers and tenants of the hills were all dependents of their greater neighbors, willing hangers-on of a system which, if they but knew it, could give them no promise of better things. The reasons for this dependency were two: many of these ne'er-do-wells were but the distant cousins of the rich, the cast-offs of the fast-growing cotton aristocracy; many others were prospective planters, hopeful that they or their sons might migrate to some new cotton region with a little store of savings, preëmpt a tract of government land, buy a slave or two, and set up as planters. It was from such classes in Virginia or the Carolinas that many, if not the majority, of the great cotton-planters had come. The lower South was as yet too big for these farmers and tenants to entertain and nurse the hopeless envy that cankers our own industrial life. They were not altogether contented; but they were far from dangerous. Moreover the planters were a democratic folk in their manners. They were too near the poor in point of time and descent to hold their heads as high as their social prestige might have tempted them to. They endeavored consciously to make and keep friends with their poorer neighbors — for these neighbors had the ballot. They were the "freemen" to whom every returning member of Congress must make his appeal against

Yankee tariffs and Yankee abolitionists; and their votes had made possible the annexation of Texas and the war with Mexico, by which the power and even the riches of the planters had been greatly increased. The lower South was a social unit except for the poor slave, of whom our knowledge comes only through the writings of his master.

The two millions of blacks on whose sturdy shoulders this kingdom of cotton was securely fastened were inexorably bound to the system. Willingly or unwillingly, they increased its solidarity and lent enchantment to the life of the planter. They boasted of the limitless lands of their masters, of the incomparable horses of "ol' massa," of the riches of "ol' massa's" table and the elegancies of "ol' massa's great house." What their inmost thoughts were is not likely ever to be known. They certainly produced the greater part of the cotton and sugar of the South; they disliked the whites who did not own slaves; and they were even more cordially disliked by those same whites. And this mutual dislike tended to fasten the bonds of slavery more closely and to prevent any rift between the planters and their less fortunate white brethren by keeping the slaves loyal to their masters and by deterring the poor whites from sympathizing with any abolitionist movement. Every class of Southern society, therefore, was disposed to lend power and influence to the owner of great plantations, save only a bare remnant of mountaineers who were too remote to feel the kinship of the masters or the racial antipathies between lowland whites and blacks.

The ancestors of these mountaineers were the pioneers of Revolutionary times who had pressed into the mountains of Alabama, Georgia, and even South Carolina, men of tough fiber and hardy natures, men who bore some of the best colonial names. There in the mountains they had remained. Their ideals were still those of 1776, and their practices were those of social and economic equality. To them the Declaration of Independence was a reality and Thomas Jefferson the greatest man of all history save one. They lived in isolated valleys, on the sides of fertile mountains, or on the banks of roaring streams. They spent a great part of their lives in hunting and fishing, and they distilled their corn and fruits into strong liquors just as the western Pennsylvanians had done in the time of Washington. They did not like the great planters; and their leaders in the various legislatures were often courageous opponents of the plantation system. But they were too few to impede the course of events. They were wayward obstacles in the path of progress, mere annoyances of the great ones of earth. Their cultural isolation was complete.

The roads that led into the mountain districts that these men inhabited were very poor, often mere bridle-paths. The great roadways had left the mountaineers undisturbed, for they connected one river settlement with another. The more important of these roads passed from the older South through Camden and Columbia to Augusta and Savannah, or through Charlotte, Greenville, Atlanta, and Montgomery. A highway known far and wide was that which passed from Louisville through Nashville into Alabama at Huntsville on the Tennessee River, and thence over the mountains to Montgomery and Mobile. A branch of this road set off from Nashville toward Memphis, whence it ran parallel to the Yazoo River, and so on to Natchez. All this Alabama and Mississippi region was, of course, connected with Louisiana and Texas by similar highways which passed through Memphis and Vicksburg. It is therefore clear that all important roads led to the great cotton districts.

This tapping of the cotton belt was also carried on by the railroads which were built during the two or three decades preceding the Civil War. The mother-road of all was the Charleston and Augusta Railway, which was the first to tap the Georgia cotton belt. Another and more important railway was projected from Augusta to Atlanta and thence to western Georgia and Montgomery. An extension of this road was then built to Chattanooga and thence to Memphis, thus binding together the Tennessee valley and the cotton belts of Georgia and South Carolina, with an outlet to the sea at Charleston. Another railway was built from Savannah to Macon, Georgia, and thence to Montgomery, with offshoots into the fertile cotton counties on either side. Thus two systems connected the eastern cotton country with the seaboard. They ran almost parallel, but the crops of cotton were so abundant that they both received ample support.

Two great roads also passed through Mississippi from north to south — one connecting Mobile, Memphis, and Cairo, Illinois, the other connecting New Orleans and Memphis. The cotton belt east of the Tombigbee was closely bound to Charleston and Savannah; the region west of the Tombigbee was bound by two systems to Mobile and New Orleans. All were better connected with the grain and stock country of the Middle West than with the Middle States and the East. A map of these roads and communications is a map of the cotton belt. The railway, that mighty maker of events, tied together the various planter sections and supplemented the river systems which had given the lower South its start in history. Everything thus tended to make the remote mountaineers dependent on the richer counties, and little was done to open the way for them to enter into the great family of planters.

The same influence and factors tended to bind the older tobacco-growing sections of the South to the masterful cotton communities. The tobacco counties of the three States of North Carolina, Virginia, and Kentucky contained about one-fourth of the population of those States, but their crops were worth, in 1850, $10,000,000, and in 1860, $20,000,000. This was the money-making crop of the region, and a very large portion of it was sold in the lower South. Both master and servant chewed tobacco or "dipped" snuff in excessive quantities. The tobacco was manufactured into "plugs" or "snuff" in Richmond and

Danville and was shipped south in long caravans of covered wagons much resembling the Conestoga wagons of Pennsylvania and the western plains. But as the railroads came into their own just before the outbreak of the Civil War, these overland trains steadily lost their trade.

What they lost, however, in tobacco they gained in whisky, which was distilled in ever-increasing quantities in the mountains of Virginia and North Carolina. Loaded with casks and crocks filled with the corn and rye whisky or the peach and apple brandy of the high and remote mountain fastnesses, these wagons gathered in trains as they approached the rich cotton belts. It was an interesting spectacle to see at eventide the lank and wiry forms of the drivers and owners of the so-called tobacco wagons as they built their fires on the outskirts of Southern towns or on the roadside to cook their next day's rations. Their great up-country horses, tethered to fences or the limbs of trees, fed upon oats while their masters ate bread and bacon, drank deeply from their jugs of liquor, and ended each meal with liberal quids of tobacco. These were the nomads of the South, the mediators between the tobacco-growers and the corn and rye whisky producers on the one hand, and the cotton-growers on the other. In return for the tobacco, the whisky, and even the home-woven cloths of the back country, the cotton men gave raw cotton for the Carolina and Virginia mills which were already rising in the larger towns, as well as coffee and trinkets for the households of the remote districts where people knew of the planters only through the tales of their wagoners and these welcome evidences of their existence.

Another commercial group not much talked of but ever present at sales, on railroad trains, and on steamboats, bound together even more closely the articulate elements of the lower South and the older tobacco States. These slave traders had either offices or agents in every black district of the older South. When a planter died, failed in business, or divided his estate, they plied a profitable trade. And why not? If it were a positive blessing to own slaves, how could it be a sin to buy and sell them? Negroes were bought and sold for the lower Southern market, driven over the long highways to Alabama or Louisiana, and sold for whatever profit there was in the business; but if droves of negroes could be gathered at such places as Norfolk or Louisville, they were stowed safely in the holds of ships and were finally discharged at the great slave marts of the cotton country. Some of the returns for cotton which might have been placed on deposit in the banks of New Orleans or Mobile thus found their way to Virginia or Kentucky and helped to bind together the interests of planters everywhere.

From Tennessee, Kentucky, and the Northwest, cattle raisers, pork packers, and drovers of mules also turned south for their best markets. Wheat, corn, and oats accompanied the mules and steers upon their journeys, for the lower South did not then produce sufficient grain for home consumption. Consequently the great highways, the railroads, and the steamers all pointed southward, and the north-bound traveler met droves of mules, hogs, or steers going to Charleston, Augusta, or Montgomery. Cotton goods or bags of cotton, sugar, and coffee, and sometimes cloths from Manchester or edged tools from Sheffield, came back in payment. While this trade did not bind the lower South so firmly to the Northwest, it did tend to bind the Northwestern farmers and merchants to the lower South, for the chief, if not the only, market for mules was in the South and it was the plantation negroes who consumed vast quantities of salt meat.

Even the merchants in Baltimore, Philadelphia,
New York, and Boston felt in a somewhat similar
way the influence of the cotton region. Their ship-
ments to the lower South grew with the increasing crops of cotton, and Eastern banks carried
for Southern merchants large deposits with which
they were loath to part when the time of reckoning
came. This strong economic pull was strengthened
by a greater social influence: wealthy young men
of the East went to the homes of the planters for
their wives, and ambitious young slaveholders in
the cotton belt married in Philadelphia, New York,
and Boston. The best families of the older communities of the North had much Southern blood
in their veins, and the first families of the South
had quite as much Northern blood in theirs. Henry
Wise, an ardent pro-slavery man, had married
a Sergeant of Philadelphia; James Chestnut of
South Carolina was half Pennsylvanian; Mrs.
Jefferson Davis was the granddaughter of a Governor of New Jersey; even the Roosevelts of New
York named their children for their Barnwell
kin of Charleston. Stephen A. Douglas married
a North Carolina heiress who owned a plantation
and a hundred slaves in Mississippi. A powerful
Senator from Indiana was the owner of a slave

plantation in Kentucky. Every such union added to the power and the sway of the cotton-planters.

So attractive were the profits and the allurements of the wide-spreading cotton fields that thousands of men and women living outside the cotton belt invested in farms or plantations, according to their financial resources.[1] In North Carolina, Virginia, and Maryland there were men in almost every county who owned plantations or parts of plantations in the cotton belt. In Lynchburg, Richmond, Norfolk, Washington, and Baltimore there were scores and even hundreds of men who drew their incomes from the cotton fields. If the present easy and flexible corporation system had been developed and applied to cotton-growing before 1850, it is very probable that very much greater sums of eastern capital would have found investment in lands, slaves, and cotton.

Such were the economic forces which were focused in the lower South and which magnified the self-importance of planters when they appeared at Newport or Saratoga. Not only was cotton king in the lower South, but it was fast extending its sway over old States like Virginia and over great

[1] This is a subject which needs investigation by some painstaking student of American social and economic life.

commercial centers like New York. Why might not planters aspire to rule the land and direct the policy of nations beyond the Atlantic? And this was just what they determined to do. Only they would set their own house in order before they invaded other lands.

As the cotton lands showed alarming signs of exhaustion, the planters concerted plans for a more scientific agriculture. The heavy rainfall of the lower South gradually washed the best soils of the uplands into the rivers, and the unending plough-ing and harvesting of cotton on the same lands tended to destroy the productive capacity of great areas. Red "gullies" and wide "old fields" cov-ered with broom sedge spoke in emphatic tones of the need of a better system of cultivation.

To remedy the evil of this condition of the land, Edmund Ruffin was employed by South Carolina to teach her planters a better way. In other States rotation of crops, shading of the hard pressed land, conserving of forests and unexhausted soils were the talk of every planters' gathering. Local, state, and sectional societies were organized to check the evil. Men who had said that "no agricultural staple has ever produced so great an effect upon the civilization of the world as cotton," now felt that if some reform were not effected the decline and fall of the cotton kingdom was as certain as ever had been that of the Roman Empire, the history of which they read with deep interest.

The remedy which they proposed was remarkable, if not revolutionary: the South should enter purposely upon a career of manufacturing.

The planters know that their production of cotton is at a sacrifice which looks to ruinous consequences because the substance of their land is annually wasting away. The remedy which we now insist upon is for the planters to resolve that the cotton mills shall be brought to the cotton fields; that they have been paying toll to the English mill long enough. The cotton fields of the United States, extending from the Atlantic to the Rio Grande, embrace in their wide extent 500,000 square miles. The interest of all planters in this great field is the same. State lines are imaginary when the sacrifice of cotton-growing labor is the question; old issues in politics may rest in forgetfulness; and the whole South may act as one state in giving a prosperous direction and division to the labor of the best-trained, most efficient, and regular force of workers on the face of the globe. But a part of this force must be taken from the soil and put into the mills. Spindles and looms must be brought to the cotton fields. This is the true location of this powerful assistant of the grower.[1]

[1] J. D. B. De Bow: *Industrial Resources of the Southern and Western States,* vol. I, p. 229.

If this manufacturing were to be brought to the lower South, negro labor would be used. And this was tried in South Carolina and Georgia with results that were more than ordinarily satisfactory. In 1852 in the Saluda mills at Columbia, 128 slaves and children of slaves were employed to run 5000 spindles and 120 looms. The cost per laborer per annum was only $75 as against $116 for the white laborer of the North. Nor was this an isolated experience. By 1860 Southern mills consumed nearly 200,000 bales of cotton per year. Woolen mills were established in Virginia and North Carolina. Eastern capital was already seeking investment in such establishments, and skilled laborers and managers from New England and Europe were waiting to put up machinery. The up-country and piney-woods whites were seen to be valuable as future labor reserves.

Thus the needs of the South, the warning of failing lands, the plentiful supply of cheap labor, and the abounding water-power were about to start the cotton-planters upon a course of conserving their lands, manufacturing their own cotton, and employing profitably thousands of poor whites who had not been accustomed to work more than a few months in the year. If the new movement should prove successful, it was thought that cities would grow up, that greater markets for live stock would be created, that rotation of crops would become the rule, that soils would be fertilized and preserved, and, what was more important, that the lower South would complete her monopoly — for the planters would have no competition from the cotton of Egypt or India, and they would at the same time keep the manufacturer's profits and all the freight charges for themselves.[1]

With things taking this turn, Southern leaders saw, or thought they saw, manifest destiny beckoning to them in Mexico and Central America. Their institutions were apparently the best in the world, their economic position incomparably the best, and their future beyond the power of man to imagine. Cuba and Mexico were in the hands of weak and backward peoples, and the poor Central American States were in still worse plight. None but selfish Englishmen could wish to stay the hand of conquest in those regions, and all true friends of mankind must wish the guiding hand of Anglo-Saxon slaveholders to be applied to Indian and

[1] It was not so clearly perceived that these Southern interests would become similar to those of the North and that Southern politicians would cease their war upon the protective policy of the industrial States.

half-breed owners of those rich and inviting communities. After the Mexican War and its easy successes, this imperialist ideal captured the imaginations of most of the leaders of the lower South. The more the world demanded cotton, the more the natural increase of the slaves enriched the planters, the more glowing the picture of a future cotton empire appeared.

Thus the trend of events in that great region which extended from Texas to Baltimore and from the Gulf and Atlantic coasts to the Alleghany Mountains, even to St. Louis and Kansas City, seemed to confirm the planter in his industrial monopoly and to strengthen his hold upon his slaves, upon his lands, and even upon the poorer whites. The master of a mansion, a cotton plantation, and a hundred slaves was undoubtedly the social model of the lower South, and he was fast becoming the arbiter of the fortunes of his section, if not of the United States as a whole. Such men and such groups seldom live long without developing a philosophy which is at once their apology and their guide to life.

CHAPTER III

THE impassable barrier between master and slave and the growing distance between the gentleman of family and the poor white inevitably brought men to the formulation of a doctrine of life peculiar to these conditions. But never in any country was it more difficult than it was in the ante-bellum South for writers to publish or believers to avow a social faith which contradicted the Declaration of Independence; and the farther southwest one went the more difficult, for democracy was too recent a fact and the open profession of personal superiority too offensive.

The discrediting of Jefferson did not begin to take effect in the lower South till such great Virginians as John Randolph and Chief Justice Marshall had successfully ridiculed his teachings as glittering fallacies. Four years after Jefferson's death, the Virginia constitutional convention openly disavowed the equalitarian teachings which had underlain the politics of the South since 1800; and two years later, when the Nat Turner Insurrection was under discussion in the Virginia Legislature, a young teacher at William and Mary College appeared before the committee on abolition and presented a new system of social science. This man was Thomas R. Dew, a trained political scientist, recently returned from the German universities where he had been taught that the inequality of men was fundamental to all social organization. He argued so forcibly against emancipation of the slaves that men began to say aloud what they had long believed — that Southern society was already sharply stratified and that men might as well avow it.

Dew did not at the beginning attack the older ideals of America. To have done so would have been to alienate men whom he must win. The Jefferson myth was too strong, even in aristocratic Virginia, for men to proclaim their own superiority and keep straight faces. Consequently Dew treated historically the mooted subject of negro slavery. He showed that slavery had been the condition of all ancient culture, that Christianity approved servitude, and that the law of Moses had both assumed and positively established slavery. If Moses and Paul justified and preached slavery among people of the same race, it was incomparably easier to convince an increasingly orthodox society like that of the South that it could be no sin in white men to hold black men in bondage. How much easier to justify the idea of negro servitude to men who had inherited their slaves from honored ancestors, when it was made plain that the Bible taught that even white servitude was right and proper! It was a time when men, especially Southern men, were studying their classics afresh. The ancient world became a real world to the South in the period of 1850 to 1860. The new philosophy not only found its justification in the writings of the greatest men of antiquity; it fitted the facts of Southern life.

Dew made it perfectly clear that slavery was as profitable to Virginians as all knew it to be to cotton-planters farther south. He insisted that the sale of the surplus supply of slaves brought almost as great a return each year as their greatest crop, tobacco. Thus to the argument of history was added that of economic profit. And here no less a person than the late Governor of Virginia, William B. Giles, came to the aid of philosophy.

Giles had proved from the figures of the custom-houses of Virginia that the returns from negroes shipped South every year were very large.

With the facts of history, the support of Christianity, and the teaching of economics in his favor, it was less difficult for Dew to attack the "fallacies" of Jefferson and the great Declaration. Besides, had not all the greater sons of the Old Dominion recently declared that manhood suffrage, equal representation, and equal rights were inadmissible doctrines? Certainly Marshall, Madison, Randolph, Tazewell, and the rest had both argued and voted against all these things. The public mood was therefore favorable, and the new faith gained a quick and ready hearing.

The new philosophy asserted that men were not equal, but that some men were fit only for the hard toil of the field while others were plainly designed for the easier task of managing and directing the labor of others. There were no natural rights; rights were prescriptive and they implied an equivalent, a service rendered to society. A landowner might vote; he had a stake in society, and he aided men by adding to the goods that men must have. One who did not own land might or might not vote, according as society directed. A

slave enjoyed the right of protection against vio-
lence, hunger, and extreme cold, and in exchange
for this protection he gave himself, his work, and
his children.

If society were organized on this basis, there
would be three classes, with well-defined rank and
standing: the highest or the guiding and teaching
group; the traders and free laborers and perhaps
small land-owners from whom the skilled labor
necessary to all groups was to be derived; and the
slaves or "mudsills," as they soon came to be called.
Professional men — lawyers, physicians, preachers,
and teachers — were expected to be recruited from
the small farmers and even from the wealthier class.
If every man remained in his place and performed
the task expected of him, there would be the greatest economy of effort and the highest civilization
possible to man. Woman would be the noblest figure of all and she would cast over men the spell of
her influence; gentlemen would be chivalrous and
knightly, devoting their best thought to the State
but always lending a hand to the weak and the
humble as the first duty of the strong.

This new teaching might not have succeeded
so promptly if men had not already been living
for years upon such an understanding of things

without being bold enough to formulate a theory. Because Dew went one step farther and put into writing the facts upon which men had acted, he was hailed as a master. William and Mary College made him its head, and students from the lower South hastened to the old institution to sit at the feet of the new Gamaliel.[1]

The principle of all this teaching was stated thus by President Dew: "The exclusive owners of property ever have been, ever will and perhaps ever ought to be the virtual rulers of mankind. . . . It is the order of nature and of God that the being of superior faculties and knowledge, and therefore of superior power, should control and dispose of those who are inferior. It is as much in the order of nature that men should enslave each other as that other animals should prey upon each other." But Dew probably did not intend to put the case so harshly as it appears in the last sentence.

It remained for Chancellor William Harper of the Supreme Court of South Carolina to advance the doctrine to its extreme form. The South Carolinian

[1] Dew's philosophy first appeared in Richmond in May, 1832, in pamphlet form. But his ideas were reprinted in the newspapers in all parts of the South and his pamphlet was reprinted many times before 1860. It is most available now in *The Pro-Slavery Argument*, Charleston, 1852.

rejoiced in the "able statement" of the case
by the Virginian and he endeavored to elaborate
the new philosophy where it seemed necessary to
the upbuilding of a perfect state. Harper's work,
which first appeared in 1838 under the title of
A Memoir on Slavery, was less historical but more
to the point than that of Dew. The Bible and the
ancient philosophers were of course the great
witnesses.

Harper conceived of slavery as the natural order:
"To constitute a society a variety of offices must
be discharged, from those requiring the very
lowest degree of intellectual power to those requiring the very highest. It should seem that the
endowments ought to be apportioned according to
the exigencies of the situation. And the first want
of society is leaders. The first care of a state which
regards its own safety, prosperity, and honor
should be that when minds of extraordinary power
appear, to whatever department of knowledge, art,
or science their exertions may be directed, the
means should be provided of their most consum-
mate cultivation." But to others such careful
training could have no significance. "Odium has
been cast upon our legislation on account of
its forbidding the elements of education to be

communicated to slaves. But, in truth, what injury is done to them by this? He who works
during the day with his hands does not read in
the intervals of leisure for his amusement or the
improvement of his mind. If there were any
chance of their elevating their rank and condition
in society, it might be a matter of hardship that
they should be denied those rudiments of knowledge which open the way to further attainments."

Not only does Harper hold that the lowest class
in society is to be trained to only the hardest toil,
but he also believes that its members are necessarily
on a low moral plane: "A slave has no hope that
by a course of integrity, he can materially elevate
his condition in society, nor can his offense against
honesty materially depress it, or affect his means of
support or that of his family. Compared to the
freemen he has no character to establish or lose."
It is not different in the relations of the sexes and
for the same reason: "In northern communities
the unmarried woman who becomes a mother is an
outcast from society. She has given birth to a
human being who is commonly educated to a
course of vice, depravity, and crime. It is not
so with the female slave. She is not a less useful member of society than before. She has not

impaired her means of support nor materially impaired her character or lowered her station; she has done no great injury to herself or any other human being. Her offspring is not a burden but an acquisition to her owner. The want of chastity among slaves hardly deserves a harsher name than weakness."

The chasm between this lowest class of society and the masters and leaders who are at the top is so great that none can bridge it. There is, to be sure, a free or intermediate class from which the truly noble are recruited and from which is derived the connecting link between the field hand and the gentleman. Men of this group are to fill the places of mechanics, merchants, engineers, physicians, teachers, lawyers, preachers, and overseers. They should be educated at the expense of society, should have the right to vote and to bear arms, and should be made to feel the pride of race and color and to appreciate the benefits of a caste system. And thus Chancellor Harper comes, like President Dew, to repudiate the doctrine of the great Virginia statesman and philosopher: "Is it not palpably nearer the truth to say that no man was ever born free and that no two men were ever born equal, than to say that all men are born free and

equal? . . . Man is born to subjection. . . .
The proclivity of the natural man is to domineer
or to be subservient." It is through the evolution
of men in society that each man or class of men
comes to find the proper place and level, and
society then crystallizes and legalizes the resulting
differences. This is the very condition of the development of civilization. Laws are made to prevent outbreaks against this established order as
well as to render the different classes contented
and even ignorant — for "if there are sordid,
servile, and laborious offices to be performed, is it
not better that there should be sordid, servile, and
laborious beings to perform them?"

But there will inevitably be resentment and insurrection: foreigners will foment troubles, natives
will be restless, and slaves may rise, in spite of the
fact that slavery tends to decrease friction more
and more as population becomes denser and the
hope of liberation from a given state of society is
definitely abandoned. To meet all contingencies,
standing armies must be created and maintained.
In the South such a course would be easy because
the honor of defending one's country would be
allowed only to white men, slaves being possible
material only in dire necessity. In the South,

"like ancient Athens, it will be necessary that every citizen should be a soldier. . . . And perhaps a wise foresight should induce our state to provide that it should have within itself such military knowledge and skill as may be sufficient to organize, discipline, and command armies, by establishing a military academy or school of discipline."[1]

It is hardly necessary to develop farther the ideas of Dew and Harper. They prepared their premises carefully and boldly. They did not speak the language of the politician, but they spoke rather as wise men giving their fellows those fundamental propositions from which practical leaders might make what deductions exigencies required. Certainly the South would no longer profess devotion to the notions of freedom and equality if these teachings should find acceptance.

Acceptance, indeed, these teachings readily found. In 1837 Calhoun, the greatest and sincerest of all Southern leaders, openly announced that he held slavery to be a positive good and that

[1] Harper's philosophy may be found in *The Pro-Slavery Argument* already cited. I have not given page and line, because I have had to make many extracts and condense them. The reader who would understand this philosophy in its minor details as well as in outline would do well to read the works of Dew and Harper.

Southerners should no longer apologize for it: "I hold slavery to be a good; . . . moreover, there never has yet existed a wealthy and civilized society in which one portion of the community did not in point of fact live on the labor of the other."[1] This statement might have been taken at one time as a peevish thrust on the part of Calhoun at the captains of industry who were getting the better of him in national legislation. But in 1837 Calhoun, like so many other Southerners of the old Jeffersonian democracy, had changed his mind; he meant what he said; he believed in the caste system of which in the South slavery was the mainstay. In his view nothing could be more unfounded and false than the opinion that all men are born free and equal; inequality was indispensable to progress; government was not the result of compact, nor was it safe to entrust the suffrage to all.[2]

These are the views to which the people of the lower South were being converted. The adoption of this point of view marks a revolution in Southern thought quite as remarkable as the revolution which took place in German thought under the

[1] Richard K. Crallé: *Th Works of John C. Calhoun, 1853–1856,* vol. II, p. 630.
[2] *Ibid.,* vol. I, pp. 8, 12, 46–58.

leadership of Bismarck during the second half of the nineteenth century. In the lower South the influence of Calhoun was very great; but even that influence could not have availed had it not been for the difficult and apparently insoluble problem of negro slavery. After Calhoun became the advocate of caste and inequality, it was not difficult for others of lesser note to follow his lead or for the great majority of the planters to accept the new faith. Still, if the lower South were to present a solid front, all the professional men and the upper middle class must also yield their belief and accept as final the idea that society must be divided into sharply defined ranks, and that some men must be the burden bearers for the rest and labor all their lives without the hope of improvement or more compensation than their food and shelter. If we examine the writings of some of the other spokesmen of the South, both lower and upper, we shall see how far this revolution of thought went.

In South Carolina nearly every leader, whether in politics, religion, or education, upheld slavery and endeavored to reply in positive terms to all who condemned the system. Macaulay, Dickens, Mrs. Trollope, and Harriet Martineau were answered with the statement that modern industrialism was worse than slavery. James H. Hammond, one of the moderate and very popular followers of Calhoun, published a series of letters in 1845 in which he attacked England and New England for the cruelties of their industrial system. As no reply was made to the heart-rending picture which he drew, the lower South took great consolation in the belief that their caste system was not as heartless as that of their opponents. Southerners, they said, did take care of the children of slaves; they did employ physicians for their sick or aged dependents; and they did maintain a sort of comradeship with their slaves which blunted the keen edge of servitude.

From this point the advance was easy to the position already taken by Dew that the negroes were the happiest of mankind, because relieved of all care for themselves and their offspring. Hammond urged that "our patriarchal scheme awakens the higher and finer feelings of our nature. It is not wanting in its enthusiasm and its poetry." William Gilmore Simms of South Carolina, author of as many books as Scott himself, lent all the weight of his name to the thesis that slaves were the happiest of laborers. William L. Yancey of Alabama made the Southern social system the theme of his marvelous oratory. Henry S. Foote, Jefferson Davis, John Slidell, and every other public man of the lower South became ardent advocates of the newer faith. Before 1850 the older Jeffersonian ideal was totally abandoned, and the contrary ideal of the inequality of men had been adopted.

To men whose interests were those of masters of slaves and whose philosophy was the doctrine of social caste and prescriptive rights, it was but natural that Walter Scott's famous novels should make appeal. One New York publisher said he sent Scott's works South in carload lots. The *Lay of the Last Minstrel* and the *Lady of the Lake* stirred Southern men to think of themselves as proud knights ready to do or die for some romantic ideal; and the long list of novels from *Waverley* to *The Fair Maid of Perth* seemed to reflect anew the old ideals of fine lords and fair ladies whom Southerners now set themselves to imitate. Scott's gentlefolk always talked and acted in lofty fashion; the poor and the ill-placed were rough and brutal, without finer feeling, and ready to accept the kicks and cuffs of their betters; and the money-getter was always the sharp and unlovely creature who suggested the Yankee pedler or crafty financier.

Before 1850 it was good form for Southern gentlemen to place Sir Walter Scott's novels on their library shelves and for all Southern boys and girls to read these books as the great models of life and good breeding. Few men ever had a greater influence over the cotton-planters than the beloved Scottish bard and novelist.

But while Scott was enthroned in every library, the sturdier Scotsman, Thomas Carlyle, also knocked at the door of Southern intellect. Carlyle went roughly to his point. "Would you turn out slaves, like horses, to graze?" Then why talk of abolition? "Every man is created to work, some at menial tasks, some at higher callings and others, as God-given heroes, to lead mankind." In scores of books and essays the grim old teacher laid out his doctrine of social subordination and class distinction. That was all that Dew and Harper and Calhoun and Hammond desired. The greatest realist in England had weighed their system and found it just and humane. It is astonishing how greatly Carlyle influenced the world. A few years later he was one of the prophets in Prussia, and his *Frederick the Great*, the first volumes of which appeared in 1858, made capital for the Hohenzollern as well as for every other imperialist the world over.

In the South George Fitzhugh took up the idea of strong-arm government, definitely acknowledging his indebtedness to Carlyle, and presented to the country a book which was designed to round out all that had gone before. In *Sociology for the South*[1] he laid down a plan for his section of the country which he expected to see adopted elsewhere if it proved successful. After restating the caste system of Dew and his successors, he attacked Adam Smith with ridicule and relentless logic. Society, he maintained, must be organized for positive, not negative, purposes. Men must be restrained, governed, subjected to discipline; and states must take care that every man, woman, and child shall have a vocation and useful employment with due support. The idle must be compelled to work — only people must not confuse with idleness that leisurely thinking which is the work of philosophers. In such a state, freedom of movement, of trade, or of industry is not possible; social efficiency and economic success in a world of reality demand organization.

But organization connotes slavery for the ignorant and the poor. In England, the duty of the state is to subordinate the owners of the mills to

[1] Published in Richmond, 1854.

the Government, and the Government should find them employees. The workers should be made slaves of the industrial lords and compelled to labor. They should be forbidden freedom of movement and should be attached to their masters, who in turn must be compelled to give them support and kindly treatment. Children should be reared at the expense of the industry. Strife and poverty must disappear. The same program should be adopted in New England and in the West. Instead of the Federal Government giving away lands or selling them in small tracts, great tracts should be granted to responsible men, who should be allowed to entail these at death upon their oldest sons. The landless and the idle of the Eastern States should be attached to these plantations and become the tenants of their masters for life.

"Slavery will everywhere be abolished or everywhere be reinstated" was the alternative presented by Fitzhugh. He expected that slavery would be everywhere reinstated and that all the world would become like the South, except that the South would have the happy advantage of making all white men free and of leaving the drudgery to negro slaves who were especially created for the purpose. With such a system, Southerners would be the happiest as well as the most favored people under Heaven. In the South all white men would be educated at public expense and the best of them would become philosophers and litterateurs, like their prototypes in ancient Athens. Women would become, where they were not already so, the queens of earth. There would be no Miss Martineaus, no Madame de Staëls, but womanly women whom men would adore, and knightly men to whom women would cling like vines to sturdy oaks. To be a Southerner would be a distinction.

With this ideal state duly propped and bolstered with laws of primogeniture and entail, and protected against free trade and foolish ideas from without, it would be impossible for other nations to compete. White men would run away from the North just as negroes ran away from the South, in order to join the new régime and to enjoy the freedom and blessings of the most intelligent and beneficent social order that the world had ever known.

In this new civilization Christianity should become the one and only religion. Slavery and Christianity were mutual supports and mutual guarantees. Under their influence property would bear all the burdens of society and its owners would receive all the honors. There would thus be no poverty and little crime because the chief motive to crime is poverty. Few men would ever become insane because every man's task would be congenial and the free open-air life would be healthful. If this system were left alone, there would be no commotions and no wars; and over and above all God would preside, and order would rule without a flaw or a slip.

While this book did not command the immediate attention that similar books in modern Germany have received, it was accepted by the newspapers as pointing the way to the future. In the most serious reviews it was treated as a great and profound work. If criticism was offered, it was always in the way of improvement and elaboration. An enlarged if not improved edition was brought out two years later under the title of *Cannibals All; or, Slaves without Masters*. Fitzhugh became an influential publicist, corresponded with Carlyle, gave lectures in the East, and set forth his doctrines till the thunder of the guns at Fort Sumter announced that the argument was closed.

This social philosophy, elaborated and constantly reprinted in newspapers or pamphlets, represented fairly what the articulate South was ready to go to war for. There was, however, some protest. The editor of the *Southern Literary Messenger* insisted in the beginning that Dew's ideal society was by no means ideal to him; it was not until 1843 that he became a convert to the new faith. In North Carolina slavery had never won such complete ascendancy as it had in the lower South; and there opposition to the accepted dogma was strenuously voiced till hushed by law or by a too powerful public opinion. In 1846 Daniel R. Goodlow, in a pamphlet of real acumen, urged that slavery was not a perfect institution. He insisted that the investment of some billions of capital in the ownership of labor was a doubtful speculation. The land would be worth as much if the negroes were free, and the capital invested in slaves might better be put into improvements.

A less effective protest was voiced by Hinton R. Helper, in 1857, in the *Impending Crisis of the South*, a book which became a campaign document in the North three years later. Helper endeavored to show that the planters composed a far-reaching oligarchy, if not conspiracy, against the poorer farmers and the landless classes. His statistics were well calculated to prove further that this conspiracy had been the sole cause of the economic backwardness of the South. But Southerners did not suffer his book to be read. A hapless agent who endeavored to circulate it was quickly haled to court. Neither Goodlow's argument nor Helper's outcry had any appreciable effect in stemming the tide of pro-slavery teaching. Not one man in a hundred even heard of them. Nor was the moderate reasoning of George M. Weston's *The Progress of Slavery in the United States* (1857) effective. Even if men in their reflective moments were inclined to agree with him, the aristocratic and feudal evolution had gone too far.

During the twenty-five years which had elapsed since Virginia had declined definitely the task of abolishing slavery and since Dew had offered his convincing argument, the cotton-planters as well as the sugar and tobacco growers had definitely and finally broken with the Jeffersonian ideal. Their growing economic power and the attractiveness of their labor system had confirmed them in their view that government must needs represent property and privilege and that democracy was a failure. Since the planters were the articulate element in society and the small farmers and landless groups were hardly in a position to assert any contrary views, it was not difficult to make the lower South socially solid. No newspaper of any importance, no college or university professor, no prominent preacher, and no politician of any party offered effective resistance. In two or three instances professors did go so far as to support mildly anti-slavery views, but they were removed from their positions. One eminent man in Charleston stood alone and was left free, apparently because any attempt to curb him might advertise his moderate ideas. The mails were closed against abolition books and newspapers as a matter of course; and boycotts were urged against Northern periodicals if they printed articles that displeased the South. There was the most perfect agreement ever known in Anglo-Saxon history. Men thought the ideal social organization had been found. Were not the planters prosperous, the middle-class and landless groups contented, and the slaves the happiest of living men?

CHAPTER IV

THE home of the cotton-planter was a modest country house of ten or twelve rooms. It stood upon an elevation along the roadside or upon a river bluff, surrounded by half a dozen or more negro cabins known as the "quarters." There were tall, spreading trees, graveled walks, shrubs, and, in the grounds of the greater places, marble figures of wild animals or replicas of antique statues. The house itself was likely to be surrounded by long porches which gave protection against the intense heat of summer but which darkened the halls and rooms of the mansion. These porches were often as tall as the house itself and their roofs were upheld by rows of huge white columns, which gave even a second rate or "tumble-down" place a grandeur that was supposed to impress the visitor and proclaim the dignity of the master and the size of his estate.

Inside the house there was a wide hall and an ample stairway leading to another hall on the second floor. From the hall on the first floor one entered the parlors, the library, and the dining-room; on the second floor were the living-rooms of the family. Ceilings were high everywhere, and windows tall and wide; but carpets were of plain design, when there were carpets at all. On the walls there were portraits of worshipful ancestors, a steel engraving of George Washington, a battle scene of the Revolution, and a painting of Calhoun or Clay addressing the United States Senate. Furniture was as a rule plain but somewhat massive. Of servants there were always plenty and to spare, for the number of servants rather than the elegance of the outfit advertised the wealth and dignity of the family.

A half-score of sons and daughters, a tall, lank, and rather weatherworn gentleman, and a slender, soft-voiced, weary-looking mother composed the family group, unless one counts the inevitable guest or old-maiden cousin who, like the furniture or the servants, always formed part of a planter's household. Though it was not good form to labor with one's own hands, yet both master and mistress knew how to perform most of the work that was daily done by the blacks. The younger members of the family took pride in their immunity from the work that is the lot of most men. Soft hands and ignorance of the vocabulary of labor and trade were considered especially becoming. Nor was the toil of the fields or drudgery of the house more attractive then and there than now and here. The injunction of Holy Writ to "multiply and replenish the earth" was obeyed; but the truth that "in the sweat of thy face shalt thou eat bread, till thou return unto the ground" made little appeal, for was not the negro created by God to do the work of the white man? His skin was black and proof against the heat of summer; he delighted in the streaming rays of torrid suns; and he preferred to sleep at noonday with his face to the sky. Negro women made beds, cleaned houses, and cooked the meals of the planters, while negro boys and girls served them at table in the great dining-room. Horses were groomed and harnessed, cows were fed and milked, and morning fires were made by negro hands. If one wanted a glass of water, a servant was ready to bring it fresh from the well; if flies disturbed the guest, and flies always disturbed everybody, there were boys to fan them away and to keep the atmosphere in motion.

In return for personal service the negroes were supplied with cabins — one for each family. These cabins were built of logs, the crevices daubed with clay, and the roofs made of clapboards or shingles. There was one broad fireplace at which meals were cooked and served and clothes were washed, and around which the little negroes gathered when the weather was cold or rainy. There were beds and mats and quilts for sleeping accommodations. Some slept on the beds, some on the floor with their feet to the fireplace, and some in the attic. There was no waste space in a negro cabin.

The slaves raised pigs and chickens, and had gardens in which they grew sweet potatoes for themselves and, in the upper South, tobacco plants in the fence corners about the "quarters." Every week the master allowed each grown person four pounds of meat, a peck of meal, and a quart of molasses, with something over for the little ones. The rest the slave was expected to find for himself — the Sunday chicken, the "greens" from the garden, and the potatoes from the cache in which they were stored away from the cold. The older slaves were allowed to keep dogs and to hunt coons and 'possums at night and, now and then, squirrels and rabbits by day. The negro is even now the

inveterate enemy of the rabbit. Little negroes
played and romped in the "quarters," in the barns,
and even in the great house; they climbed the
tallest trees, and they put their black faces out of
every window of the cabins when visitors were
around. Their clothing was like the annals of the
poor, short and simple, merely a shirt which
reached to the knees. Shoes and hats were useless
encumbrances for youngsters in winter as well as
in summer. Older negroes received a new suit of
clothes, two pairs of shoes, and a cheap hat each
year, and at Christmas time a little liquor, some
trinkets for the women, and a small sum of spend-
ing money. Masters and servants lived much together on the smaller plantations, and white and
black children played together whether on great
places or small.

It was a community life. Each member felt
closer to the others than is now generally supposed.
When the old master or the old mistress died,
there was genuine sorrow in the "quarters" and a
long train of black mourners followed the remains
to the grave, for the break-up of plantations was
as distressing to slaves as to their owners. When
slaves died, their remains, neatly dressed, were
laid away in plain coffins in the "God's acre"

of the plantation. The death of a slave was lamented as much in the mansion as in the "quarters," and every attention was given the sick. Indeed the oversight of the health of the slaves, always ignorant and sometimes reckless, was a burden of life which the mistress seldom evaded. Family physicians attended negroes as well as masters; and on great estates there were chaplains to bury the dead, to officiate in plantation chapels, and to ask blessings at the planter's table. But the white chaplain was not popular with the negroes. They preferred to sit in the galleries or annexes of the white churches or to worship under the guidance of their own preachers where white people did not intrude, and where they could, under such auspices, indulge without restraint in weird chants, bodily contortions, and loud shrieks.

If the master was niggardly in the matter of dress for his slaves, he was also rather indifferent about his own clothes. It had long been a mark of distinction in a gentleman of Virginia to dress in shabby or last year's suits; and what was good form in the Old Dominion was good form in the cotton country. Nor were the women fastidious. Elegant silks and gay bonnets then, as always, delighted their hearts, but the tyranny of seasons and of fashions did not rule the plantations. In Washington, however, where Southerners were always on dress parade, at Saratoga, or at the Virginia springs, planters' wives followed the Parisian styles, wore costly jewels, and drove handsome equipages. There the absentee mistress of even a small number of slaves was at her social best, and her dinners, her salons, her balls were "the rage." One thinks here of Mrs. Stephen A. Douglas, Mrs. Jefferson Davis, and Mrs. William Gwin, the wife of Senator Gwin of California.

In Charleston, Mobile, and New Orleans men of business, lawyers who owned country estates, and merchants whose names were known in New York and Boston, were more careful to maintain the fashion and dressed more like the Prince of Wales than was the custom on the plantations. After all, the democracy of Jefferson was waning, and in these centers the women generally dressed, much as they do today, to display the riches of their husbands; they were living advertisements of the family standing. To drive at six o'clock upon the Battery, to dance at twelve o'clock at St. Cecilia's, and to have a pew at St. Michael's were evidences of success that none could have misunderstood.

Travel was a part of every Southern planter's

life. Before the day of railroads the family carriage was an institution. Large, cumbersome, swung high on suspension springs, it rocked and rolled along the rough roads of the lower South with all the dignity of a limousine and with much more picturesqueness. It was trimmed with brass and gold and usually had the family coat of arms adorning the doors. There were light metal steps on which the ladies mounted and which were pulled in when the door closed, leaving the un-initiated wondering how the precious freight was loaded on or off. The horses were groomed and harnessed in the best of style, and high upon the box sat a majestic son of Africa, the happiest product of the plantation system. Such an outfit one might see any day upon a lonely country road making its way for miles or hundreds of miles to visit neighbors or kindred in distant States.

Sometimes these Southern gentlefolk were on their way to New Orleans or Charleston to see the races. In summer they were likely to be seeking the way to Pass Christian for the Gulf bathing beaches or else they wandered farther away to the mountains of North Carolina, in order perchance that the planter might take part in a caucus of South Carolina politicians. But wherever they

went they stayed weeks or months to get the worth
of their long journey. To travel all the way from
Alabama to Old Virginia was no small undertaking
even to the tough and wiry frames of our ante-
bellum planters and there was therefore much
necessary hospitality on the way. If one may
believe some of the contemporary accounts, however, there was often a good deal of querying and
wagging of heads when the outriders, the drivers,
and the horses, not to mention the gentlemen and
ladies who clambered out of these overland arks,
all settled down at a distant cousin's for a month's
sojourn.

Still, all was not plantation routine, dress, and
travel. In the great house there was a library
which was likely to be the home of law books, of
histories, of English novels, and of handsomely
bound Greek and Latin classics. There were
quarterly reviews on the library tables; and a file
of the Charleston *Mercury*, the New Orleans
Picayune, or the Richmond *Enquirer* stood on the
lower shelves of the bookcases. The debates in
Congress were read everywhere, for Congress was
the arena in which great Southerners displayed
their talents and endeavored to thwart their rivals

and opponents from the North. The most sacred of all public documents was the Constitution of the United States, which many could repeat verbatim from start to finish. But South Carolinians alone felt the necessity and the duty of remembering two constitutions at all times and upon all occasions.

The Virginia Bill of Rights, the Virginia and Kentucky Resolutions, and Madison's Report of 1799 were only a little less sacred to *emigrés* of the Old Dominion in the lower South. Of course, New England periodicals gave place to the *Southern Review*, published in the sacred Carolina city, to *De Bow's Review* of New Orleans, and especially to the *Southern Literary Messenger*, which always brought with it something of the atmosphere of Richmond and was hardly less dear to the Southern heart than Charleston itself. But while the *North American Review* and the *Knickerbocker Magazine* seldom gained a place on Southern tables, *Harper's Magazine* and, just before the war, *Harper's Weekly* found many readers in the South.

While law and propaganda held large places in the thought of the lower South, there was time and interest left for the lighter literature which so many men have regarded as a test of culture —

belles-lettres, as the people of 1850 were prone to say. Walter Scott's romanticism and hero-worship suited their taste and braced their social system, as we have already seen, and he furnished matter enough for the longest of the idle days of a lonely cotton plantation. *Marmion* and *Ivanhoe* and the *Heart of Midlothian* were common intellectual property in all parts of the South. Yet Byron with his reckless love of the lawless and, later, Thackeray with his quiet but effective irony won the hearts of readers. In fact, every English writer of standing made an appeal to the planters so long as he did not attack their beloved institution of slavery. The planters were consciously returning to a former allegiance. It was the English, not the budding New England, literature which won them, although Charles Dickens with his tearful stories was too much for Southern digestion; and on his Southern tour in 1859 this great author fortunately did not pass beyond Richmond.

If ladies and gentlemen of the cotton kingdom liked to read the better English writers, they also readily turned to the older classics. Doctor Johnson and Oliver Goldsmith and, above all, Shakespeare were found upon every shelf and were read and reread for their content as well as for their form and style. The plays of Shakespeare were presented in Charleston long before they found a hearing in Boston and Philadelphia; and Richmond, Mobile, New Orleans, and Memphis readily furnished large audiences for the greater English playwrights even before those cities became populous. Planters who had been educated at the University of Virginia or who had traveled in Europe took up their winter residence in the nearest cities, in order to enjoy the art of the elder Booth, who made his American début in Petersburg in 1821, or to hear the *Barber of Seville*, given in New Orleans every winter, or to sit in Charleston for portraits by the painters De Veaux and Fraser. Although New Orleans was the first city in America to give serious attention to opera and always maintained close ties with Paris, Southerners did not develop their love for music, painting, or sculpture beyond the level of the amateur.

Aside from portraits which they liked to have made for their ancestral halls, some promising efforts at sculpture, which made a beginning in Richmond before 1860, and the mere pleasure of hearing good music, the planter's taste for the fine arts made little progress. His life did not lend itself to that form of expression. To be sure,

Gottschalk was born in New Orleans, and there was an Academy of Design in Charleston; but the former never counted America his musical home, and the Academy had only a fitful existence.

From Thomas Jefferson, who enjoyed his Homer to the last year of his long and busy life, to the Rev. Dr. Benjamin Palmer of New Orleans, planters of both the tobacco and the cotton-growing regions held firmly to the old idea that a liberal education could not possibly be based upon any other foundation than the languages and literatures of the ancients. Perhaps they received this idea from their European ancestors; or, like Goethe in his old age, they may have rediscovered Rome and Greece. Whatever the cause of their early liking for the classics, the preachers of early Presbyterianism, missionaries trained in the methods and the theology of Princeton, carried Latin and Greek wherever they went. They prayed in English but kept their Greek grammars in their pockets, and every aspirant for education or leadership in the Southern backwoods was set to work on Latin forms and Greek roots. In a hundred log "colleges" during the first thirty years of the nineteenth century, Southern youths labored over their classics from sun to sun, like the slaves in the fields.

Calhoun, McDuffie, and scores of other well-known leaders, were the product of these schools. Both preachers and politicians made long quotations from Virgil and Homer and Horace to prove their education and to practise their learning. Young men wrestled with pronunciation and old men spent their spare hours in the shade of friendly oaks mastering the thoughts of Plato and Aristotle in the original. At social gatherings and at even graver meetings men wrangled about the correct renderings of passages from their favorite authors.

In such an atmosphere as this it is not surprising that the colleges of the lower South long remained essentially schools of Greek and Latin. Yet men could not write popular books or political harangues in the languages of Homer and Cicero, even though they did assign ancient names to thousands of their political pamphlets. The challenge of Irving and Cooper and Hawthorne was constantly before them, and even the most loyal of the classicists felt this new pull away from their toilsome pages. Aside from the serious reviews already mentioned and the excellent literary pages of the better daily and weekly papers, Southerners felt that they must produce fruits worthy of their civilization if they would stand unabashed in the presence of the rest of mankind.

The greatest and best of the cotton-planter poets and novelists was William Gilmore Simms of Charleston (1806–1870), who at the age of twenty published his *Lyrical and Other Poems*. This volume, however, fell flat from the press and found no response from the severely classical gentlemen of Charleston who measured everything by the standard of "Mr. Pope" or "Mr. Dryden." Simms tried again and yet again — a score of times — till more than twenty volumes of verse came from his pen. Though he imitated the vein now of Scott, now of Byron, he somehow failed to attract the planters. Then Simms tried the writing of novels, and in 1834 he published *Guy Rivers*, which yielded him a small bank account. The next year he brought out two other works, *The Yemassee* and the *Partisan*, each of which passed rapidly through two or three editions and made his name known in London better than in the lower South. Although the planters felt the need of a native literature and even organized clubs for its encouragement, they did not read enough contemporary books to recognize the merit of one of their own writers when he appeared.

Simms himself, though perhaps the only Southerner in all ante-bellum history who could say so, complained that the fact that he earned his living by his pen prevented his recognition in the best Carolina circles. It was a curious contradiction in the planter life; but Simms continued his efforts to give the South a native literature until he was the author of nearly a hundred volumes and until he was recognized in both North and South as a great writer. To be sure, his romances reminded one of Cooper and even of Scott; still, the subjects were Southern, and many of his characters were original and charming and one or two were unsurpassed. When the great war came he was living in style at his country place, a great library around him and guests always at his table. What more could one ask?

Of less importance but distinctly a planter in character was John Pendleton Kennedy (1795–1870) whose *Swallow Barn* (1832) and *Horseshoe Robinson* (1835) portrayed planter life and Carolina ideals in ways that gave their author as much recognition as could be afforded by men who were very busy with their negroes and their politics. Although the writings and the methods of Kennedy are remarkably similar to those of Irving, there was enough originality in these works to entitle them to much more attention than they now receive. The pictures of country life, of the 'squire of the county court, of the mistress of a plantation, and of great neighborhood dinners are delightful and bear more than a single reading. So well was his talent recognized in England, we are told, that Thackeray asked Kennedy to write the fourth chapter of his famous *Virginians* and tradition has it that the request was complied with.

Good though the work of Simms and Kennedy was, the best of the planter South was found in its poetry. Aside from minor lawyer-poets and the miraculous *My Life is Like the Summer*, of Richard Henry Wilde, the lower South produced two men of genius — Timrod and Hayne, who were inspired and trained by Simms in Charleston, although it took the disasters of the Civil War to bring out their greatness.

Troubled all his life by poverty, lonely beyond the fate of most mortals, and stricken for many years with tuberculosis, Henry Timrod (1829–1867) hastened to his grave without having done half his work. His *Cotton Boll*, *The Lily Confidante*, and *Vision of Poesy* show the artist of more than mere talent. But the times were out of joint and

when peace came he was exhausted. His equal
was never produced in the lower South.

Although his friend Paul Hamilton Hayne
(1830–1886) wrote more and had the satisfaction
of seeing his works more frequently in bound
volumes, he was hardly the equal of the author of
The Cotton Boll. Hayne published three volumes
before 1860, and he lived to bring out in Philadelphia and New York still other volumes after
the great struggle was over. Because in all these
works he speaks as a Southerner he ultimately won
from English critics the title "Laureate of the
South." But the great planter régime never quite
recognized him, nor were his royalties drawn from
their purses. Like Simms, he clung resolutely to
his section and defended its cause and ideals to his
dying hour. But he defended them in a lonely
cottage in Georgia where he spent the last twenty
years of his life earning his livelihood in the "sweat
of his brow," seeking still to give aid now and
then from his slender stores to his more unfortunate friends, Timrod and Simms.

But Simms, Timrod, and Hayne were after all
only echoes of that greater world of literature of
which Scott, Byron, and Dickens were the masters, and they belonged by tradition to English

literature. There was a more original and therefore more important group of writers who lived in
the lower South and who finished their work before
the war began. The chief of these were the Rev.
Augustus Baldwin Longstreet (1790–1870), William Tappan Thompson (1812–1882), Johnson
Jones Hooper (1815–1863), and Joseph G. Baldwin
(1815–1864). In 1834 Longstreet published, in
sportive mood, his *Georgia Scenes*, in which he
portrayed the homely life and fun of the poorer
white people of the lower South.

Longstreet made the fisticuffs, the cock-fights,
and the horse-swappings of county court days the
subjects of his writing, and few have equaled him
in his chosen field. His neighbor and partner in
the management of a rural newspaper, William
Tappan Thompson, published in 1840 *Major
Jones's Courtship*, which continued the same kind
of work. This book won immediate success, and
its homely scenes the simpler folk in all parts of
the South still remember. Of less importance but
well worth reading is Johnson Hooper of Alabama.
Hooper made the rascally, trifling fellow who
swindled his neighbors or ran away from his family
his special favorite, and *Simon Suggs* is his best
creation.

Of a higher order was the work of Joseph G. Baldwin, also of Alabama, who made Virginia his especial field in a series of articles which he published in the *Southern Literary Messenger*. That Baldwin had read Irving is perfectly plain; but his treatment of Virginia subjects and characters is so original and mirth-provoking that few can read his pages today without enjoyment. It was a sort of second Knickerbocker's tales which he finally gathered together and published under the title of *Flush Times in Alabama and Mississippi* (1853). It was not so much character-sketches as humorous description which Baldwin presented.

In this group of writers one sees today the predecessors of Mark Twain — whose parents, in fact, came from this very region. The grotesque and the absurd are here the special veins of men who seek not to teach men anything nor to show that the South could produce a literature. What they saw and heard in their daily intercourse with common men they endeavored to reproduce in book form. A half a century later Mark Twain and Bret Harte, doubtless familiar with their works and living among people essentially similar, followed up their methods and won international repute.

After all, the life of the plain people of the lower South is more important than that which displayed itself in the great houses, at the races, or at the resorts. This life was not altogether so crude and raw as Longstreet depicted it, nor was it so much out of sympathy with the planter ideal as Frederick Law Olmsted represented in his *Seaboard Slave States* (1856) and *Journey in the Back Country* (1860).

The farmers and the tenants, the piney-woods people and the mountaineers were like farmers and tenants elsewhere. The larger number of them lived in fairly comfortable log or frame houses of one or two rooms. There were few pretensions to beauty of situation or elegance of outfit. The house stood upon the roadside, by a fresh-flowing spring, or among the great pine trees. The door was so roughly made that it creaked on its hinges, dragged across the floor, and had to be fastened with a latch which was lifted from the outside by a string put through a small hole. The wide fireplace, here as in the negro cabin, was the center of all family activity. By its side stood a great crane which swung back and forth the large pots and kettles for cooking the greens, bacon, and mush, the staples of Southern middle-class fare. The crane was the object of wonderment to small boys who loved nothing better than to set it in motion and hear its strange but comforting song as it was pulled from over the crackling fire. In the chimney-corner there were a grindstone, a scythe, and a great bundle of broom straw tied against the wall and kept out of the rain. In this living-room the mother of the half score of farmer's children did her work day in and day out, cooking, washing, and ironing for the growing family. She was the first to rise in the morning and the last to retire at night.

If the family owned a negro family, a single cabin was provided near the larger one, and there in miniature the life of the master was re-lived from day to day, except that the farmer's wife tended the black children as well as her own, in order that every one who could might work in the fields with the stalwart farmer and his sons. The life of such a master and such a slave was hard and monotonous — the harder and the more monotonous in proportion as the master was more or less "on the make," for the ambition of such a man was to be the owner of a big plantation.

There was little in such a household that suggested books and papers or politics and religion.

On the plain board table which stood in the center
of the best room there was a big family Bible with
possibly a copy of Bunyan's *Pilgrim's Progress* by
its side. From the joists were suspended bags of
seed-corn, dried fruit, and great pods of red pepper;
there was a great pine chest in the corner in which
the best quilts and home-woven counterpanes were
securely kept against the day when "company"
came; over the door hung the rifle and by its side
the powder horn which had done service at King's
Mountain or even in the border wars of Scotland
in behalf of Cameron or McDougal clans.

Outside the house was the kennel with always
two or three dogs which, added to the neighboring
hounds, readily made a pack for a chase after fox
or deer. The barns and stables were built of logs
and were none too large or comfortable for the
stock. Chickens, ducks, and pigs were always to
be found and there was constant noise, now of one,
now of the other, clucking, squawking, and squeal-
ing each according to its kind. The garden was
large and fertile. From it came cabbages, potatoes, beans, and roasting ears in abundance for
both whites and blacks; and there were flowers
along the borders, a pear tree in one corner, and
a great scuppernong arbor in another. If there

were no great cotton crops, there were enough corn, potatoes, pork, and fowls to feed a numerous family.

Another and a lower grade of society lived on the waste lands and pine barrens and among the remote mountains. Of this life Olmsted writes *con amore*. It was less wholesome and less promising than that which has just been described. Larger families lived in small and dirty cabins where all slept in one room. Beds were filthy and filled with vermin and the floors were often the common mother earth covered with trash or straw. These people showed little ambition for the larger plantation life and little hope of personal or family betterment. They were contented to hunt on the lands of the planters, to fish for shad in the streams, and even to steal from the herds of their richer neighbors. Their dress was not unlike that of the slaves. Not a solitary book adorned their houses, nor were the morals of these illiterate whites higher than those of slaves. Reading and writing were as good as lost arts to them. The visitor or stranger who happened to pause at their cabin doors was stared at with curious and inquisitive eyes. To such a family a five-dollar piece was a rare thing indeed; but whisky was so common that rough and fatal duels were fought on sight. There were the inevitable gun and powder horn, the lean and hungry hound, and a few chickens and ducks. There was usually a single stable which housed an aged horse, and there was certain to be a pig in a filthy sty.

Among the farmers and tenants, the poor whites and mountaineers, there was indifference toward the great planters of the South but no real hostility save in remote highland districts; and even the hostility of the mountaineers waned as improved means of transportation brought them into touch with the planters. Never did these highland folk, however, assume a friendly or sympathetic attitude toward the slave. The so-called "crackers," "red necks," and "hill-billies" had not as yet come to hate the negroes, for they little thought that these would ever be freedmen; but the embers of hatred smoldered, ready to be fanned into flame in later years, after the South had been scourged by war and transformed by an industrial revolution.

Altogether the people of the lower South were not unlike those of other sections. The great planters and landowners compared favorably with the industrial and commercial princes of the East. Their ideals and their culture were taken as the

standard of the cotton country; their houses, their
liveries, their dress, and their manners were the
best of the time.   Like wealthy men of all ages,
they cultivated the arts in an amateurish fashion;
they loved to sit to artists for their portraits,
and they liked to read good books or at any rate
put them upon the shelves of their libraries.   It
was even a boast of the most enlightened of them
before 1860 that the planter was not only a reader
of books and a patron of authors, but that he was
himself a dabbler in *belles-lettres*.   What, indeed,
might the cotton kingdom not become if left to
work out her own destiny?

CHAPTER V

RELIGION AND EDUCATION

CONTRARY to a common preconception, the people of the lower Southern States were sincerely religious, although at the beginning of their development as a peculiar section of the country, they had little patience with what was called revealed religion. From the University of South Carolina, where many of their teachers and models of propriety were trained, there came the strong deistic utterances of Dr. Thomas Cooper, famous on two continents. Cooper was counted one of the great spirits of his time. Young men from all the cotton region flocked to his institution, where they heard him lecture on the Pentateuch after the critical manner of recent years. He was perhaps the first teacher in this country to break down the faith of men in the literal inspiration of the Bible. South Carolinians liked the scientific spirit which took nothing for granted — at least that was their attitude in 1819.

Of greater importance was the example of Thomas Jefferson, who had all his life been known as a deist. Late in his career Jefferson founded the University of Virginia with the intention that no religious creed should get a hearing there. A strong agnosticism prevailed for many years after his death, until the growing religious conservatism of the Virginians compelled the new University to take to its bosom the representatives of the leading churches as guides and monitors of its students. From still another center the new country received quite unorthodox, if not deistic, opinions. Transylvania University, "a seminary of true republicanism," was located at Lexington, Kentucky. Its president, Horace Holley, although a New Englander, was practically a deist. Among his four or five hundred students there were always many young men from the cotton States preparing themselves to be lawyers, physicians, and teachers.[1]

[1] The Roman Catholics of New Orleans, whose easy-going methods suited some twenty or thirty thousand merchants and planters, contributed their mite in the direction of religious orthodoxy. In New Orleans, Baton Rouge, and Mobile there was a nucleus of Catholicism that might under better skies have won a controlling influence in large districts of the cotton kingdom. It did not so fall out, however, and the Catholics remained one of the minor denominations of the planter civilization.

It is still said in the South that, although there may be other roads to the Celestial City, no gentleman would choose any but the Episcopalian way. It may be doubted whether there were twenty thousand Episcopalians in all the region from Charleston to Galveston at the outbreak of the Civil War, yet members of "the church" were almost invariably found in the seats of the mighty, of governors, congressmen, and magistrates. St. Michael's Church in Charleston was the Westminster of the cotton country; and to be buried in the sacred soil of that parish was almost as good as to be alive in less favored provinces. In Savannah, Montgomery, Mobile, and New Orleans, the gentry belonged to the good old colonial church whose clergy were not so pious themselves as to be disagreeable father confessors. To own a handsomely bound prayer-book and to occupy the family pew once a year was evidence enough of one's religious regularity, even though one did hazard great stakes in the Charleston races. No curate thought less of his patron for his interest in this sport.

The hard work of saving the souls of common men was left to such leaders of other denominations as the Presbyterian preachers who had for half a century taught the up-country farmers the shorter catechism and the Greek roots. Since the late colonial days young and muscular Christian missionaries, nourished upon Calvin's *Institutes* and Virgil's *Æneid* at the College of New Jersey, poured into the Southern up-country. They preached their stern and unbending doctrine on the Sabbath, and on week-days they set scores of young men to work upon the classics. From sunrise to sunset these earnest seekers after knowledge pored over their Greek and Latin, convinced that the salvation of their souls depended upon the memorizing of thousands of heroic lines or upon explaining to their masters the intricacies of languages that had not been spoken by any considerable number of people since the fall of Constantinople.

Men and preachers trained in these schools were not likely to endure very long the presence of such philosophers as Thomas Cooper or to manifest continued devotion to the inconsistencies of such dilettante rationalists as Thomas Jefferson: they must know the ground they stood upon. Once they had won over the small farmers of the hills in the two Carolinas and Georgia, these teachers of a sterner faith were in a strategic position when small farmers became big cotton-planters with scores of slaves about them. They took command in these three States before 1840. Presbyterians became governors and members of Congress without waiting for the consent of their religious seniors. The president of the University of North Carolina was a Presbyterian divine, for all the world like the good Dr. Witherspoon of Princeton. In South Carolina President Cooper was brought to trial for his "shameful atheism" in 1834. He was found unfit for his high position and promptly turned out to graze at eighty years of age! John H. Thornwell, a student of Cooper's, was one of the powers behind the movement and not many years passed before he was himself the president of the University. Not to be outdone in the matter, Thornwell founded, in the very shadow of the University, the Southern Presbyterian Theological Seminary, where young scions of old houses could thenceforth be instructed aright in the vital doctrines of the great Genevan.

From Cooper and Jefferson to Thornwell and Calvin was a long road to travel in two decades; but the South Carolinians went the whole distance without knowing that they had moved from their first position. What South Carolinians did was

good form, and other Southerners were likely to
follow suit. Even the great Calhoun became interested in Calvinism and manifested a genuine
concern in the growing religiosity of the planters.
But the Calvinist meat was too strong for babes.
While the Presbyterians put poor Cooper to rout,
gave the professors at the University of Virginia
anxious nights, and sent President Holley hastening away from Lexington, they did not hold the
more illiterate Southerners of the hills to their way
of thinking. A planter might be a good Presbyterian; but a "cracker" or a "red neck" found
the Princeton faith too drastic. He grasped with
difficulty the doctrines of the divines. Presbyterianism, moreover, grew more aristocratic as its
members became more wealthy and better educated. A denomination which furnished governors
and presidents of universities could not have its
preachers shedding tears in the pulpit and inter-
lining their hymns for ignorant congregations.

So the larger part of the work of saving souls
fell to Baptists and Methodists. From the days of
Daniel Marshall and his wife, half-illiterate men
had traversed every county of the South and had
preached in bush arbors to thousands of "dying
men and women," whom they called back to fullness

of life. In the backwoods of South Carolina, Georgia, and the other cotton States these earnest, God-fearing men preached and prayed, wept and sang, till thousands of the neglected were made conscious of their individual existence and of their social importance. There were three or four hundred thousand of these converts and recruits, some from the planters of the coastal plains, more from the farmers of the hills, but most from the poor and remote settlements where people were out of touch with the currents of the times. Before 1860 about a million of the people of the lower South were connected with the churches, and of these the vast majority were Baptists and Methodists.

Meantime a great social transformation had taken place in the lower South. In the beginning nearly all these people had been opponents of slavery and of all forms of privilege. But, as farmers became planters and landless men became farmers and owners of their "labor," opposition to slavery and privilege almost disappeared. Even the masses of poorer people and church members became defenders of the existing régime. While the Catholics and the Episcopalians had been content to let civil affairs take their own course and had

promptly adjusted themselves to the social strati-
fications which they saw about them, the other
denominations had at first protested and then had
gone into the highways and the hedges after the
inarticulate masses of men, only to find in the end
that both they and their converts became, like
their older religious brethren, conservatives and
owners of slaves.

The Methodist and Baptist denominations had
wrought a similar work in the North. Their missionaries carried the Gospel to the East and to the
rising West. Jesse Lee, Peter Cartwright, Jonathan Going, and their kind preached and wept
and sang in New England, the Middle States, and
the Northwest until the common people were
won. Cartwright said that the power of the Devil
was fairly overcome in Illinois and Indiana before
1860. Literally millions of small farmers and men
without property joined the new churches. As
time went on most of these men became well-
dressed, prosperous citizens, conscious of their
worth. In the absence of the institution of slavery
in their midst, they kept to the early idea that the
holding of men in bondage was a sin, but they were
not disposed to attack the South because of its
slavery.

In 1843 Orange Scott, a very able preacher of New England, stirred the consciences of his Methodist followers on the subject of slavery in much the same way that Garrison was stirring the minds of deists and agnostics. But the leaders of the denomination refused to be stirred. Scott then withdrew from the church and carried with him fifteen thousand earnest followers. The menace was so great that in 1844, when the national Methodist conference met in New York, although there were other things to be done, the one thing that all men thought about was the healing of the schism. This, however, could not be done unless the Southern Methodists, who composed at least half the church, yielded to the demand that they give up slavery. The test turned on the case of Bishop Andrew of Georgia, whose wife owned slaves. The discipline of the denomination had declared from the beginning that no preacher should own slaves. Andrew was a bishop who must minister to the churches even in New England. He must either give up his wife's slaves or give up the work to which he had been ordained and in which he was a master spirit. It was a hard alternative. The Southern Methodists chose to defend and maintain slavery and to make Andrew's case their own;

the Northern Methodists took the view of Orange
Scott and William Lloyd Garrison. Both parties
were friendly but in deadly earnest. They sepa-
rated. They could not do otherwise, for the
people of the cotton States would have banned
forever any preacher who attacked slavery, and
the Methodists of New England, at any rate,
would have refused to countenance a clergyman
who endorsed slavery. The Methodist Church
South was therefore organized in 1846, with
Joshua Soule of Ohio as its leading bishop.

From the date of the separation to the outbreak
of the Civil War the Methodist Church increased
as it had never increased before. The membership
doubled in fifteen years. Preachers like McTyeire
and Capers and McSparran became as well known
to the lower South as leading governors and congressmen. McTyeire published a little handbook[1]
which taught what the true relations of masters
and slaves should be. Dr. William A. Smith of
Virginia, who was very influential in the cotton
States, argued in a book which was widely discussed that slavery was divinely established and
that it was the duty of all good men to defend it.

[1] H. N. McTyeire: *Duties of Masters and Servants* (Premium Essays
of the Southern Baptist Publication Society, Charleston, 1851).

Preachers owned slaves; planters guided the polity of the church; and the Bible became the arsenal from which the best pro-slavery weapons were drawn. And as all men had now accepted the total and absolute inspiration of the Bible, the thrusts of these weapons were not easy to parry.

What happened to the Methodists happened likewise to the national Baptist organization. When in 1844 the Baptist Foreign Mission Board, sitting in Boston, refused to send a slaveholder as a missionary, Dr. Basil Manly, a leading Baptist preacher who was also president of the University of Alabama, made protest, carried the matter to the Baptist state convention, and procured the adoption of resolutions condemning the rule of the Foreign Mission Board and refusing further co-operation. The next year representatives of the Southern Baptists assembled in August and organized the Southern Baptist Convention. The best and ablest preachers of the denomination were present and guided the deliberations of the assembly. Manly, Richard Fuller, A. M. Poindexter, and the rest assumed the rôle at once of religious statesmen. In a short while they published at denominational expense prize essays on the subject of the relations of Christian masters to their slaves. The institutions of the South became the institutions of the church. Sermons and denominational influences became increasingly pro-slavery. The membership of the Baptist Church increased a hundred per cent during the next fifteen years. Clergymen were entirely at one with their planter deacons who, like their Methodist friends, governed the polity of the church.

Although the Presbyterians avoided a break in their national organization before 1861, it was not because the same influences were not at work. The clergy of the lower South quietly assumed control of the national assemblies. Dr. Thornwell, who became the real leader of American Presbyterians, was president of the University of South Carolina for a time, then president of the Southern Presbyterian Theological Seminary at Columbia, and all the while editor of the *Southern Presbyterian Review*, which was for many years one of the most influential periodicals in the American religious world. Thornwell was close to Calhoun before the death of that statesman; he was the idol of young Presbyterian preachers all over the South and the envy of those of other denominations, and there have been very few pulpit orators in this country who equaled him. Next to Thornwell

stood another remarkable figure, Dr. Benjamin
M. Palmer, like Thornwell a South Carolinian, the
idolized pastor of the largest church in New Orleans. The attitude of most Southern preachers
without distinction of denominations may be seen
in the following quotation from Palmer's Thanks-
giving sermon in 1860:

The providential trust [of the Southern people] is to
conserve and perpetuate the institution of domestic
slavery as now existing. . . . With this institution
assigned to our keeping we reply to all who oppose us
that we hold the trust from God and we are prepared to
stand or fall as God may appoint. . . . [This attitude
embraces] the circle of our relations, touches the four
cardinal points of our duty to ourselves, to our slaves,
to the world, and to Almighty God. It establishes the
nature and solemnity of our present trust, to preserve
and transmit our existing system of domestic servitude
with the right, unchallenged by man, to go and root
itself wherever Providence and nature may carry it.
This trust we will discharge in the face of the worst
possible peril. . . . Should the madness of the hour
appeal to the arbitration of the sword, we will not shrink
even from the baptism of fire. If modern crusaders stand
in serried ranks upon some plain of Esdraelon, there shall
we be in defense of our trust. Not till the last man has
fallen behind the last rampart, shall it drop from our
hands; and then only in surrender to the God who gave it. [1]

[1] Thomas Cary Johnson: *The Life and Letters of Benjamin Morgan
Palmer*, Richmond, Virginia, 1906, vol. I, pp. 210, 213.

This expression of one of the ablest and purest of Southern preachers met with wide-spread if not universal acceptance. Such unity and such complete religious organization as the lower South now presented gave every assurance of success to the program of religious education which Thornwell, Manly, and leading Methodists everywhere advocated. The Presbyterians had the greater theological schools and they exercised the greatest influence upon the collegiate teaching of the South. But the Baptists had important institutions in North Carolina, as well as Furman University in South Carolina, Mercer University in Georgia, and Howard College in Alabama. They began in remarkable fashion to build a theological school at Greenville, South Carolina, which should offer as full and thorough courses in divinity as were to be found anywhere else in the country. They raised a hundred thousand dollars for their initial endowment fund in 1857 and another hundred thousand was subscribed in the next two years. Of this movement the leader was James P. Boyce, brother of the radical secessionist member of Congress, and himself one of the richest men in the South. The Methodists sent their sons to Randolph-Macon in Virginia to learn wisdom and theology from

William A. Smith, an acknowledged pro-slavery leader. But another school of the prophets was opened at Emory, Georgia, a little while before the war began. Presbyterians, Methodists, and Baptists had finally come to one opinion about the higher education of their clergy; they were in direct control of more than half of the colleges of their section; and their spirit prevailed in all the state institutions.

It is not difficult to understand the tendency and purpose of education in a community led and guided by sincere and able religious teachers of the mold of Palmer and Manly. If they sought to give every young clergyman a collegiate and even theological training, they were not less interested in pressing upon all the necessity of higher education for the laity. The result was that in the decade between 1850 and 1860 practically every college and university in the South doubled its attendance.[1] The University of Virginia had

[1] Twice as many young men per thousand of the population were in colleges in the lower South or in some of the Eastern institutions as were sent from similar groups in other parts of the country. Eleven thousand students were enrolled in the colleges of the cotton States, while in Massachusetts, with half as many white people as were found in all the cotton States, there were only 1733 college students. Illinois, with a population of 1,712,000 or more than half as many white people had three thousand young men in her colleges. The income of all the

nearly a thousand students, young men from every cotton State with their servants and horses and hounds, as well as with their Greek and Latin texts. At the Universities of South Carolina, Georgia, Alabama, Mississippi, and Louisiana there was not only growth in numbers but improvement in the quality of the students and in the character of the courses offered. At the University of South Carolina Francis Lieber gave the best work in political science that was found in the country, and at the same time Joseph Le Conte was feeling his way to a theory of the origin of species which in 1859 made Charles Darwin the foremost of scientists. At the University of New Orleans Joseph C. Nott was giving instruction in ethnology which found expression in many scientific writings and which applied the principles of the so-called law of the survival of the fittest; nor was the work of J. D. B. De Bow as a teacher of commercial subjects behind the best of his time. The

higher institutions of the lower South in 1860 was $708,000, which represented an increase of more than a hundred per cent over the figures for 1850. The six New England States, with the best public school system in the world outside of Germany and with an accumulated wealth far in excess of that of the cotton region, spent only $368,469 per year in collegiate education, and their population of 3,235,000 sent only 3748 young men to college. (*U. S. Census 1860: Mortality and Miscellaneous Statistics*, p. 505.)

medical colleges of Charleston, Mobile, and New Orleans were already preventing young Southerners from going to the University of Pennsylvania in such numbers as formerly.

The promise of the lower South in learning and science was so great that the ablest teachers of the time were not loath to settle there. Robert Dale Owen, one of the foremost geologists of the North, was sorely disappointed when he failed to obtain a chair in the University of Alabama in 1847. And the elder Agassiz hardly knew whether to accept a position at Harvard or to remain a professor in the Medical College of Charleston, where he did some of his greatest work. Audubon did the better part of his famous *Birds of America* in the neighborhood of New Orleans, while his next great book, *Quadrupeds of America*, was in large measure the result of work he did with John Bachman of Charleston. Joseph Le Conte tells of a conversation he had with Langdon Cheves in the summer of 1858 in which the latter outlined the theory of the survival of the fittest as a principle that scientific men ought to work out.

Even if in some respects the standards of Southern colleges in 1860 can be criticized, it remains true that they had made greater progress than

similar institutions in other parts of the country.
Gentlemen had become conscious of their social
and political responsibilities. They were the favored class; they must govern, and they prepared
to do so by educating their sons as they had not
been accustomed to do before the new Southern
social philosophy was adopted or before the issue
between North and South was so clearly and
sharply formulated.

Nor was the improvement of the common schools
less significant. The greatest social theorists of
the South, Harper and his followers, believed and
taught that every white man should have an opportunity of higher education and that talent
wherever found should be subsidized by the State.
In response to this teaching the reforms of Horace
Mann in New England and of Thaddeus Stevens
in Pennsylvania were being applied by William
H. Ruffner in Virginia, which always influenced
the lower South; by Calvin S. Wiley in North
Carolina; and by the famous William L. Yancey
and President Manly of the State University in
Alabama. In South Carolina and in Mississippi
the same spirit was at work, one of the chief
reformers being the redoubtable John H. Thornwell, whose writings on the subject of popular

education are not the least creditable of his numerous activities.[1]

In the matter of illiteracy the planter civilization was in worse plight than any other section. In a population of 2,500,000 white people there were 175,000 illiterates, somewhat more than were found in States like Indiana and Illinois, although the difference is so small that one would not do well to insist upon the comparison. In the lower South distances were so great and population so sparse that the masses could not be easily reached by education. The schools were of recent origin, and books and newspapers went mainly to the plantation houses along the main currents of intercourse, the rivers, railroads, and greater highways.

But if illiteracy had not been overcome — and under post-bellum conditions it had taken half a century to make much progress — there was little

[1] Although the States were not so liberal in their grants to lower schools as to colleges and universities, yet there were 425,600 children in the schools of the cotton States in 1860. This showed that one child in every seven of the white population in the lower South was in school, at least for a short term. In the remainder of the country the ratio was one to five or five and a half. In the cotton States $2,432,000 was expended each year upon the common schools and $1,383,000 in the maintenance of academies and private schools. Comparison with Eastern conditions or with those of the Northwest shows once again that the planters were not far behind in actual performance and that they were in the lead in the ratio of progress.

crime and lunacy. In many counties jails stood
open; and in all the counties and towns the reports
showed an astonishingly small percentage of delin-
quents. The open spaces of the country gave men
free room. The criminally disposed were not in so
large a proportion as in other parts of the country;
nor did many break down under the conditions of
life and find their way into the hospitals for the
insane. The planters claimed much credit for this
favorable showing, though in truth it was rather
their outdoor life than any social arrangements
that reduced the numbers of these unfortunate
classes.

Did no kindly man rise to ask something for the
unfortunate slave? The effect of the separation of
the Methodist and Baptist churches in 1844 and
1845 stirred the preachers to give the slaves a part
of the Gospel at least. From 1845 to the outbreak
of the war, men like Bishop Weightman of South
Carolina devoted their best efforts to lifting the
negro from his slough of religious ignorance and
superstition. Churches were built on the larger
plantations; more room was prepared in the older
church buildings for the accommodation of negro
congregations; and every church had its gallery
for the slaves. But in spite of all the efforts of the

preachers to induce in them a quiet and reverential demeanor, the black worshipers would cry aloud and sometimes chant mournful songs during the services.

Sermons for negroes were not preached from such texts as "The truth shall make you free," but from such more appropriate themes as "Servants, be obedient to them that are your masters" and "In the sweat of thy face shalt thou eat bread, till thou return unto the ground." Negroes were not allowed to hold religious meetings without the presence of some white man. They might be taught to read the Bible, the Prayer Book, and the hymnals of Methodists and Baptists, but more learning was not thought good for them. The reason for this point of view requires no explanation here. If the negro did not relish having to worship frequently in the white man's church, he at least did realize that his master was becoming more thoughtful of his human interests.

CHAPTER VI

THE PLANTER IN POLITICS

THE political basis of the plantation system was the county court, and the county court of the South came from the banks of the James and the York rivers. In old Virginia a county court was composed of a group of justices of the peace meeting once a month to try petty cases of law. These justices were the grandees of their respective neighborhoods. They were vestrymen in the established church, owners of plantations, and lords of manors. Their wives were the ladies of the land and their daughters set the hearts of young blades aflame when they appeared in church. They were men of good common sense, familiar with the codes of Virginia and to a less degree acquainted with the precedents of English law courts. Everybody looked up to them; and they made themselves responsible in considerable measure for the good behavior of the countryside.

What they thought was right was likely to become law.

Now when these bewigged and bepowdered gentlemen took their seats on the county bench, the wheels of justice in the old commonwealth of Virginia began to revolve. But aside from the ordinary business of courts, they sat in administrative sessions to appoint sheriffs and road overseers and to order the building of bridges and schoolhouses. At informal meetings they determined which of their number ought to stand for election to the next assembly, passed upon the conduct of returning members of Congress, and as time went on learned to denounce the conduct of rascally Yankees. The government of Virginia during the first half of the nineteenth century rested securely upon the shoulders of the county justices of the peace.

In fact, these justices inherited their social position from honorable English ancestors who had sworn by the name of the King; or, if they were self-made men, they were duly recognized by the planter gentry as worthy of a place among them. The county bench was the source of many good things. Vacancies in the court were filled by the surviving judges; and all was done with such regard to precedent and after such deliberation that county courts seldom ran amuck. Through all the storms of the Revolution and the trials of the Jeffersonian period, these local organizations functioned smoothly and never for a moment lost their hold either upon the public or upon the course of events.

This was the model upon which South Carolina remade her judicial system when at the end of the Revolution she took into political partnership her great and growing up-country. The county courts of Georgia, Alabama, and Mississippi were but images of Virginia institutions planted upon a distant soil. Florida and Louisiana readjusted their French and Spanish procedure to fit the general model, though retaining the Napoleonic code. Texas took her system from Missouri, which in turn had taken hers from Virginia.

The justice of the peace was an institution of the lower South quite as much as of Virginia herself. To know this gentleman of the old school, this humane and good-natured autocrat, mildly proud of himself and keenly resentful of any criticism of his Latin or of his law, is to know the political life of the South as well as of the cotton kingdom, because every justice of the peace, save on the

distant frontier, was a slaveholder or likely soon
to become such, a conservative in politics and religion, and a member or prospective member of the
Legislature.

The political power of the cotton kingdom therefore was firmly lodged in the hands of successful
business men. There was never in America a more
perfect oligarchy of business men than that which
ruled in the time of Jefferson Davis and Alexander
Stephens. Laws were made by the owners of
plantations; the higher courts were established
by their decrees; governors of States were of their
choosing; and members of Congress were selected
and maintained in office in accordance with their
wishes. And, as we have already seen, they were
the ruling members of all the churches. Truly
nothing of importance could happen in the lower
South without their consent. This fact gave to
the South its unity of political purpose and that
moderation of social change which men of wealth
always prefer. Security of property, loyalty to
church, and safety in education were the guarantees of the system.

Still, there were party differences. The older
Federalist groups along the coast of Carolina and
Georgia had slowly merged into the Jeffersonian

party after it had become "safe and sane." Jackson disrupted that party and brought into power a mass of Western farmers and land-hungry tenants. At once the Federalist areas and the big black counties along all the rivers in the lower South formed a party of opposition. Though Henry Clay became the sponsor of this party, national impotence was its rôle, for no great aggressive party is likely to grow out of conservative beginnings. The Jackson "rough necks" became the sober Democrats of Polk's Administration and conservative reactionaries in the Administrations of Pierce and Buchanan. The larger planters and justices of the older counties everywhere tended to follow Clay, while the smaller planters, the rising business men, liked the rougher Jackson way. Besides, Jackson could carry the West, and the votes of the West were necessary to any aggressive national policy. But these differences were the differences of older and younger groups, not the differences of social irreconcilables. Consequently, though each party twitted the other on occasion with being disloyal to slavery, in any great crisis they were almost certain to unite, for, whatever happened, the planters felt that they must control the cotton kingdom.

If the planters controlled the lower South, they were likely to control the border States; and if they held these two sections together in national legislation, they were more than likely to guide the policy of the United States as a whole, for a compact minority with great wealth behind it and with leisure to devote to public affairs is almost certain to govern any country. That is, a population of two and a half millions in the lower South, with only a tenth of them directly connected with slavery, would guide a nation of twenty millions, nine-tenths of whom were either outspoken or silent opponents of slavery and all it connoted.

Under these circumstances the leaders of the lower South undertook about 1840 to widen the area of slavery, that is, expand the cotton kingdom. John C. Calhoun, who controlled a large following in both political parties in the eastern end of the lower South, was an ardent advocate of expansion. The young Senator from Mississippi, Robert Walker, a leader of the Jackson wing of the planters on the Mississippi and a most adroit politician, was even more ardently in favor of annexations. After some years of maneuvering the two men effected a working alliance of the cotton men of the South and the farmers of the West; and in the

Democratic convention of 1844 they committed the Democratic party of the country to their ambitious policy.   They defeated Henry Clay at the time when he had set his heart on the presidency and elected James K. Polk, who completed the annexation of Texas, declared war on Mexico, and took possession of New Mexico, California, and Oregon, in spite of the opposition of John Quincy Adams, Daniel Webster, Martin Van Buren, and Clay himself.

The success of the movement gave the planters such confidence in themselves and such prestige before the country that they felt themselves invincible.   Southern and Western volunteers offered themselves with such enthusiasm and fought over the Mexican hills and mountains with such brilliancy that Southern members of Congress declared that the whole North American continent should be seized and held.   Western Democrats like Senator Douglas of Illinois shared this vision of a continental republic.   If Jefferson Davis, just entering political life from the Southwest, was set upon making an American lake of the Gulf of Mexico, Lewis Cass, speaking for the Northwest, was equally covetous of Canada.

The imposing position of the planters in the

national life stirred the aged Adams to propose the
secession of the Northern States and caused New
England men of more sober cast of mind to con-
template that last desperate move of the defeated
party. But in the very hour of victory Polk and
his Southern supporters denied to the Northwest
the improvements which they asked for their rivers
and harbors and at the same time refused some of
their leaders appointments which were thought to
be their due. In August, 1846, Jacob Brinkerhoff
of Ohio and David Wilmot of western Pennsylvania started in the Democratic ranks a revolt of
which the defeated and sore Van Buren made
utmost use. Anti-slavery men balked at the acquisition of territory from Mexico unless it should
first be declared free soil; and planter interests
suffered many setbacks in the House of Representatives.

In the succeeding presidential election Van
Buren broke from the ranks of his party, set himself
up as an anti-slavery candidate for the presidency,
and defeated Cass, the candidate of the Democratic
party. As for the Whig party, it had only to profit by these dissensions. It nominated and elected
General Zachary Taylor, who, though himself a
Southerner, was not committed to the designs of the

planters. Although the party convention had not framed a platform, many Whig leaders throughout the campaign had declared that the area of slavery must not be extended through the aid or connivance of the national legislature. The Taylor Administration therefore was not disposed to allow the planters to reap the fruits of their success.

Balked in their plans, the spokesmen of Mississippi, duly prompted by Calhoun, gathered in a mass meeting at Jackson, their state capital, early in December, 1849. They called upon the people of Mississippi and of the other planter States to arouse themselves and defend their property and their institutions. Later the Legislature of Mississippi elected delegates to a Southern convention to be held at Nashville, Tennessee, in June, 1850. All the other Southern States responded with more or less enthusiasm. If Congress refused to allow slavery to be carried into California or New Mexico, then — according to the threat often heard — the cotton States would secede.

Scenting the danger beforehand, Clay returned once again to the Senate. He alone of the Whig nationalists had an important following among the planters of the lower South. Half the delegates to the Nashville convention proved to be his followers;

and in States like Mississippi and Louisiana there were Unionist Democrats who were not ready to break up the country merely if slavery were refused protection in California. Realizing his strength, Clay arrived betimes at the capital and set his friends to work. His reasonableness, his refusal to have relations with the President, his dislike of Seward, and his hatred of Weed, carried Democrats and slave-owners like Thomas Ritchie, the famous editor, and Henry S. Foote, an ally of Calhoun, into his party. The compromise measures of 1850 under the masterful management of Clay melted away the stern resolution of the Nashville convention before it gathered.[1] The secession movement proved abortive. The planters acquiesced in the measures of Congress, and Calhoun died, broken-hearted at the failure of his program.

At this juncture the Whigs played into the hands of their opponents. Under the guidance of Seward, the Whig party refused to accept whole-heartedly the work of Clay, the compromise which had been forced upon them, and nominated for President in 1852 a neutral candidate, General Winfield Scott,

[1] For an account of these compromise measures of 1850, see Chapter VII of *The Anti-Slavery Crusade* by Jesse Macy (in *The Chronicles of America*).

on a platform of doubt. Seizing the opportunity with renewed hope, the planters "handpicked" Franklin Pierce, accepted the work of Clay without qualification, and won the electoral vote of every State but four in the following November. The planters were now in a position to regain every point which they had lost in the compromise.

President Pierce sent Christopher Gadsden, president of a South Carolina railroad, to Mexico to purchase another strip of Mexican territory on which a great southern Pacific railroad was to be built. And he sent Pierre Soulé, a most ardent Louisiana imperialist, to Spain to purchase Cuba at any cost. There was reason to believe he would come back successful. At any rate every American diplomat in Europe was apparently counseled to lend assistance. If Soulé was successful, two other slave States would be promptly admitted. The outlook was so bright that the Secretary of State, William L. Marcy, became a candidate for the Democratic nomination of 1856 on a platform of Southern expansion.

The planters renewed their hopes, and well they might. A majority of the House of Representatives was Democratic; the Senate was overwhelm-

ingly Democratic; the President and Cabinet were
in full sympathy with the Southern Democratic
leaders; and seven of the nine justices of the
Supreme Court were either owners of plantations
or pro-slavery in attitude. The chairmen of all
the great committees of Congress were owners of
slaves and ready to initiate legislation in the interest of the lower South. Why should not the
planters, experts in government, direct the policy
of the United States?

Facts indicated that in the cotton country the
planters did set themselves this task. Their economic interests urged them on; their social philosophy and their religion gave them conscious
unity of purpose. Political unity, the condition of
immediate success, was within sight. From the
time when, in 1852, Alexander Stephens and Robert
Toombs deserted the Whig ranks for those of the
Democratic party, the political solidarity of the
planters was more definitely assured than it had
ever been under the bipartizan régime. Upon the
death of Clay most of the followers of that brilliant
politician prepared to join the ranks of the Democracy. With the exception of some sporadic resistance from Native Americans, or Know-Noth-
ings, in 1854–56, the party of Davis and Slidell and

Toombs and Stephens governed the South, and
the whole country as well, until 1860. Only a few
lonely spirits such as Andrew Johnson and John
Bell, both of Tennessee, and the famous Sam
Houston of Texas, distinguished themselves in
Congress by voting against the dominant Southerners.

But this unity depended upon an avowed
Unionist policy, not upon the dis-Union program
as put forward at Nashville in 1850. Not even
Davis himself desired separate Southern action
after 1852. The planter politicians now sought
allies in the East and the Northwest. Asa Bigler,
the boss of Pennsylvania, Tammany Hall and
John A. Dix of New York, Toucy of Connecticut,
and Caleb Cushing of Massachusetts — these were
already enlisted, while the aged Van Buren and
his son, "Prince" John, made haste to return to
their former allegiance now that Cass had been
duly punished. From the Northwest, Senators
Allen of Ohio, Cass of Michigan, Jesse Bright of
Indiana, Douglas of Illinois, and Dodge of Iowa
answered the call of the lower South. Scores of
lesser lights followed in the orbit of these larger
luminaries. Nothing succeeds like success; and
at that time the planters were unquestionably

successful in adding to their political following both in Washington and in their state capitals.

Still, the guarantee of a long lease of power at the national capital required a complete unity of purpose at home. And that solidarity was made the objective of a campaign of publicity which became intensive in 1853 and which closed only with the echoes of the big guns at Charleston in 1861. Leading governors, great planters, merchants, and editors assembled from year to year in commercial conventions at Charleston, Savannah, Montgomery, and Vicksburg to deliberate upon the interests and ideals of the lower South and of the border States as well. The conservation of cotton soils, the efficiency of labor units, the growing importance of manufactures in the South, the importation of slaves from Africa, free schools for all whites, religious instruction for the negroes, railroads to the Pacific, and steamship lines to Europe were the staple subjects of discussion.

Of the items in the program two require more particular attention here. The more important one was the building of a railroad from some point on the lower Mississippi to San Francisco. If this road were built at national expense and by liberal land grants, as Davis proposed, a tier of slave States would inevitably be set up all along the line, and California itself would be drawn into the lower Southern group. If the planter life and ideal were thus spread across the continent, the commercial interests of the Middle West and even of the Missouri valley must seek outlets through Southern ports. For the new railroads which would be built through wide regions of prairie and forest would thus open new areas to development. The Mobile and Ohio, the Louisville and Nashville, and the Illinois Central systems were already under way. If Memphis and New Orleans became terminals of the proposed Pacific system, then they, with Vicksburg and St. Louis, would become the cities of the future.

When Gadsden returned from Mexico with the assurance that enough territory could be acquired to make a Southern Pacific route feasible, the whole influence of the Administration directed by the able Secretary of War was brought to bear upon the undertaking. But Douglas foresaw the consequences of the Davis plan and hastened to defeat it by promoting a Central Pacific Railroad with Chicago as its eastern terminus. His Kansas-Nebraska bill and the consequent anti-slavery agitation of 1854 defeated the immediate ambitions of the cotton-planters; and from that date to his death the lower South hated and distrusted and feared Douglas.[1]

Of equal importance to the lower South was the problem of population and immigration. Southern conventions discussed the matter long and ably. The annual increase of population in the North due to immigration from Europe was nearly half a million. If this increase continued, no amount of solidarity and coöperation of leaders in the cotton kingdom could save that section from relative decline. At the same time, to invite a large inflow of Germans, Irish, and English laborers would endanger the planter control. Nor was it likely that foreign workers would readily settle in the South. There was little free land left, and slaves were sold at prices that made the ambition of poor men to become planters seem fantastic. Far-seeing planters, as we have noted, urged the diversion of capital to manufacturing so as to attract foreign labor and to create home markets for Southern products. But this industrial transition could not be made in a day.

[1] The history of the Kansas-Nebraska bill is recounted, with a difference of emphasis, in Chapter X of *The Anti-Slavery Crusade* and in Chapter II of *Abraham Lincoln and the Union* (in *The Chronicles of America*).

South Carolinians took up the problem of relative decline in population as early as 1855 and recommended the repeal of the laws of 1807 and 1819 which forbade the foreign slave trade. It was assumed that the laboring population of the lower South was to consist of negro slaves and must be increased by new importations from Africa. The reopening of the slave-trade, to be sure, would once have caused protest and apprehension. But the teachings of Dew and Harper, the attitude of the churches, and the attacks of the abolitionists, had dissipated all doubts and fears. The prosperity of the cotton States now required large numbers of slaves from Africa. Upon this black and stolid human foundation would the Carolinians build and expand their empire, which was to embrace Cuba, eastern Mexico, and California.

In the Southern convention of 1858 William L. Yancey appeared as the champion of the new policy. As he and his friends conceived it, the importation of hundreds of thousands of blacks from Africa would not only offset Northern importations of labor from Europe, but, by reducing the price of slaves and increasing the profits of masters, it would give poor men a better chance to share in the "blessings" of slavery and thus widen the foundations of Southern influence, and it would increase the total population and thus increase the representation of the planters in Congress. From every point of view this importation of slaves would add new advantages to those already possessed by the lower South. The great obstacle would be the opposition on the part of the North to the repeal of the laws against the foreign slave-trade. A minor obstacle was the reluctance of border States like Virginia to run the risk of losing their profits from the domestic slave-trade. If their slaves were not sold in the lower South, they would multiply on worn-out lands and become such a burden that emancipation might become necessary. But this objection was not considered to be a real one. Virginians would find in a stable and masterful cotton kingdom that which would counterbalance this disadvantage.

The objections which Congress would interpose were evaded by recommending to the States that they enact apprenticeship laws somewhat like those of colonial times and not unlike those of Illinois and Indiana in 1858. Under such laws black apprentices could be imported in large numbers and the Federal courts could not intervene. For nearly fifty years Southern and Northern slave-traders had brought blacks from Africa and had sold sometimes as many as ten thousand a year, and yet no one had ever been effectively punished. Moreover, if slavery was a blessing — as men now believed it to be — what wrong could there be in selling slaves?

Before the debate was closed at the next Southern convention, Louisiana, Alabama, and Georgia enacted laws under which numbers of negro apprentices from Africa found their way to the plantations. If these experiments proved successful, larger numbers would be imported. Of course difficulties might arise in the transfer of such apprentices, but since the benighted African would know nothing of the laws or of the distinctions between apprentices and slaves, there would be little difficulty in disposing of all as slaves. Free blacks could live in the lower South only by common consent, for the laws forbidding their presence were drastic, and they could easily be reduced to the same status as all other negroes.

Closely akin to this evasion of Federal law was the persistent Southern filibustering against Cuba and Central America. Soulé returned from Spain unsuccessful, and the brutal statement of the American attitude toward Cuba in the famous

Ostend manifesto brought reproach to President
Pierce and his advisers. But even before this set-
back Narciso Lopez had led two or three expedi-
tions against the coveted island. On one occasion
as many as six hundred Americans had been landed
and led against the Spanish authorities. A governor of Mississippi lent assistance in 1851 so openly
that he was cited to appear before a grand jury in
New Orleans; and a nephew of Senator John J.
Crittenden was killed in Cuba in the same year
fighting under the banner of Lopez. Public men
and newspapers in every Southern city commended
these movements. The greatest of all these free
lance war-makers was William Walker of Tennessee, who attacked first Mexico and then Nicaragua, proclaiming himself a deliverer wherever he
went. Twice he was arrested by the authorities
of the United States, but each time Southern Senators defended him and his doings.

These incursions into Cuba were plainly intended
to carry planter institutions to less fortunate
countries, and the best thought of the South approved the purpose. Why should there not be an
expanding cotton, rice, and sugar kingdom just
as there was a growing industrial empire in the
East and North?

The presidential election of 1856 was of primary importance. The mistakes of Pierce had made Douglas the foremost candidate of the Democrats, and the rising tide of opposition led by Seward gave evidence that the planters might soon be defeated in national politics and reduced to the necessity of secession if they intended to pursue their program unhindered. Yancey and Slidell and the other able leaders of the lower South attended the Democratic convention which met at Cincinnati in June, 1856. By careful management they prevented Douglas, their chief aversion, from winning the nomination, though his popularity at the North was very great, and they finally set up as their candidate James Buchanan, who had never "spoken ill of the South." This victory had not been won, however, without yielding to Douglas and the West the privilege of writing the party platform. It was but a restatement of the idea that the settlers in any new Territory should determine for themselves whether they would have slavery or not. It was the application to Territories of the principle of popular sovereignty which both then and later was acceptable to the up-country element in the South. Only the great planter group understood and opposed it, and above all opposed Douglas, who was always talking about the plain people and local self-government.

Few campaigns in American history have ever been more hotly contested than that of 1856. There was frequent talk in responsible circles of the cotton kingdom that secession would surely follow the election of Frémont, the candidate of Seward and the new Republican party in the North. In Pennsylvania alone something like a million dollars was spent by the two leading parties — a huge sum for that time. But the planters won. They surrounded the President-elect and made perfectly sure that no dangerous men should get into the Cabinet. The men who had directed the policy of Pierce now directed that of Buchanan; and Davis, recently transferred to the Senate, John Slidell of Louisiana, and Jesse Bright of Indiana were the powers behind the throne. The planters still had the majority of the Senate and the Supreme Court, though the House was deadlocked. It would be the duty of the President to get the country out of the tangle in Kansas, for, if he succeeded, the young Republican party, which was composed of the most heterogeneous elements, would probably go to pieces.

Buchanan endeavored earnestly to solve the

Kansas problem. In spite of some opposition from his Southern advisers, he appointed Robert Walker Governor of the distracted Territory. Walker promptly reported that the only way out of the difficulty was to let the people decide the question of slavery for themselves without let or hindrance. That was what Douglas had said all along. But such a policy would make Kansas a free State and the lower South could not surrender so easily. Happily for the Southern leaders, the Supreme Court in the spring of 1857 was of the opinion that an owner of slaves had the legal right to carry his human property into any Territory and keep it regardless of all local opposition. Under the far-reaching Dred Scott decision, it would seem to be the duty of the country as a whole, under the Constitution, to guarantee the rights of property in slaves in all national domains.

If this decision was in harmony with the spirit of the Constitution, and it certainly seemed to be, the popular notion that the people of each Territory might forbid slavery was utterly untenable. Consequently when Walker urged the President to leave the problem in Kansas to the vote of a hostile local population, the planters with one voice denounced the idea. They pressed about the pliant

Buchanan, they carried the war into Congress, and they stirred the lower South to resistance. All the debates about the importation of slaves from Africa, the futile efforts still going forward at Madrid for the purchase of Cuba, the filibustering in Nicaragua, and the efforts to procure another part of Mexican territory, paled into insignificance before the crucial question whether "a mob" in Kansas should be allowed to deprive Southerners of rights of property in defiance of the Federal Supreme Court.

While Buchanan wavered, Douglas issued a declaration of war upon the President and announced that he would carry the matter before the people of the Northwest for decision. Every Southern Senator and almost every Southern leader deprecated such a move and denounced the man who made it. But Douglas found support in the North. Republican leaders, sore pressed for a popular champion of their cause, talked of making him their candidate for 1860. The planters won the President to their side; and the choice between the two points of view went first to the people of Illinois and later to the people of the whole country. In the contest in Illinois, there arose the prophetic figure of Abraham Lincoln, the very embodiment of American democracy, declaring for simple majority rule. The decisions of the Supreme Court must yield to popular votes; laws and even constitutions must be remade to suit the wishes of simple majorities. If the Court refused, then the Court must be reconstituted; if laws gave more to slaveholders than the people wished, then laws must be repealed. Lincoln's position was that of one who appeals to the referendum and recall today, a far cry indeed from that which had led to the formation of the Union. If Lincoln had his way, the United States would become a democracy.

While Douglas won a reëlection to the Senate on the issue as he pressed it, there was in reality little difference between him and Lincoln from the viewpoint of the lower South. What did it matter to the owner of slaves whether all the people of the North voted down his rights under the Constitution or whether the same thing were done by a majority in a single Territory? The whole point to him was that no majority anywhere could deprive him of rights guaranteed by the supreme law of the land. Upon this issue, almost every planter, whether of the cotton or of the tobacco States, took his stand. Yancey threatened revolution. The South Carolina leaders, following Robert

Barnwell Rhett, a life-long advocate of secession, began to "set their house in order," expecting to leave the Union in 1860. Every prominent member of Congress from the South veered round to the position of Jefferson Davis, who had said mournfully that the cotton States might have to leave the Union, although he refused to counsel such a course. Newspapers and teachers and preachers of all the churches in the lower South declared that the submission of the rights of the planters to plebiscites was revolutionary and subversive of all law and order. They prophesied that the business men of the North would one day rue the choice they were about to make. But it was not the business men of the North who were getting nervous or unruly — it was the democracy of the North.

The rulers of the cotton kingdom prepared for the struggle of 1860 while the war of North and South went sadly on in Kansas. Congress remained deadlocked: the Senate favored the South; the House, the North. Everything depended upon the outcome of the party conventions and the election of 1860. The Democrats met at Charleston. Douglas prepared long beforehand to win a majority of the delegates to that body. He would have the convention declare in favor of popular sovereignty as the preceding convention had done with the aid of Southern votes; and then he would have the convention nominate him to the presidency. If he succeeded in both these moves, he would almost certainly be the successor to Buchanan.

To Davis and his planter followers such an outcome would be only a little less fatal than the election of a "black Republican." The cotton States could never submit to a President who juggled with the rights of property. They must first of all defeat Douglas. If they succeeded in this they might nominate a safer man and endeavor to defeat the Republicans in the succeeding general election. In other words, the planters had reached the point when they would deliberately sacrifice in the Northwest their allies of long standing rather than yield an inch in the matter of their rights in the Territories. Having vanquished Douglas, they would then meet Seward or Lincoln with the hope of further success.

When the Charleston convention met in April, 1860, a battle royal began between Douglas Democrats and the reactionary members of the party who accepted the leadership of Jefferson Davis. Neither faction would yield. When this became clear, Yancey, the greatest orator of the South since Patrick Henry, made one of the famous unreported speeches of history. He reasoned with the Northern delegates, he stirred the emotions of the crowded galleries, and he raised the enthusiasm of his planter followers to the highest pitch. When he finished, bade farewell to the convention, and took his leave, the members from all the lower Southern States followed him. The first great bolt in American history had taken place. Buchanan and Davis, still in Washington, approved; John Slidell, August Belmont, and the Tammany Hall representatives lent Yancey assistance and money; and the reactionary elements of the party in the North applauded.

The great planter machine had reached its acme of influence and power; and all the cotton country submitted to its dictation. In fact, all the articulate elements of the lower South were represented in it. This organization now moved toward the nomination of a candidate of its own. The planters met again in Richmond and nominated for President John C. Breckinridge, a moderate Kentucky politician. The Douglas men reassembled in Baltimore and nominated their hero. To the surprise of most Southern public men, the

Republicans made Lincoln their standard bearer. Still other candidates were put forward by the so-called Constitutional Union party.

Lincoln was elected. The cotton States prepared to leave the Union. Their unique culture, their still powerful position in national politics, and their remarkable prosperity were all staked upon the event. They would form a State in which the laboring class should be the property of the capitalist; they would perfect a society in which every man should have a place and every man should keep his place. In the lower South there were to be slaves, farmers, and gentlemen. There would be no poverty; nor would there be any serious disagreement on the fundamentals of society, for sermons, speeches, books, and teaching in the colleges were all to defend the existing order and to look towards its perfecting. Society in the lower South was to be the realization unhindered of the social philosophy which began with the repudiation of the Declaration of Independence and ended with the explicit recognition of social inequality. There was then no doubt of final success, and there was little if any serious protest against the ideals that were to be realized.

BIBLIOGRAPHICAL NOTE

Among the landmark contributions to the study of American history is the seven-volume work by James F. Rhodes: *The History of the United States from the Compromise of 1850* (1893–1906). An abridged one-volume version by Allen Nevins was published in 1966. Another valuable reference is Thomas D. Clark's series *Travels in the Old South* (1956–1969), comprised of the three volumes *The Formative Years, 1527–1883: From the Spanish Explorations Through the American Revolution* (1956), *The Expanding South, 1750–1825: The Ohio Valley and the Cotton Frontier* (1959) and *The Ante-Bellum South, 1825–1860: Cotton, Slavery and Conflict* (1969). William G. Brown's *The Lower South in American History* (1902, reprinted 1970) is helpful for its portrayal of leaders and methods. Other useful treatments include *The Old South* (1968) by John Osborne; Thomas P. Abernethy's *The South in the New Nation, 1789–1819* (1961); *The Militant South, 1800–1861* (1964, revised ed. 1970) by John H. Franklin; Avery O. Craven's *The Growth of Southern Nationalism, 1848–1861* (1953) and Fletcher Green's *Constitutional Development in the South Atlantic States, 1776–1860* (1930, reprinted 1971).

For a contemporary account of the economic imbalance between the South and the North on the eve of the War Between the States consult *The North and the South: A Statistical View of the Condition of the Free and the Slave States* (1857, reprinted 1972) by Henry Chase and Charles W. Sanbourn. In *Southern Wealth and Northern Profits* (1960, new ed. 1966) T. P. Kettell describes the flight of capital to bankers, merchants and shipping companies in the North. The use of Negro slaves in Southern factories is the topic of Robert S. Starobin's *Industrial Slavery in the Old South* (1970). *The Plantation and the Frontier, 1649–1863* (2 vols., 1910, reprinted 1969) by Ulrich B. Phillips contains much original material on cotton farming. *The Cotton Industry* (1897, reprinted 1974) by Matthew B. Hammond is an excellent analysis and Charles S. Davis's *The Cotton Kingdom in Alabama* (1930, reprinted 1973), a useful supplement as is *The Rise of Cotton Mills in the South* (1921, 2nd ed., 1968) by Broadus Mitchell. A related basic factor is considered in *The History of Transportation in the Eastern Cotton Belt to 1860* (1908, reprinted 1968) by Ulrich B. Phillips. Jerome E. Brooks, in *Green Leaf and Gold: Tobacco in North Carolina* (1962) tells the story of the second most important Southern staple.

A good survey of Southern life and civilization is Carl Bode's *Antebellum Culture, 1840–1861* (1970) as are two studies by Clement Eaton: *The Growth of Southern Civilization, 1790–1860* (1961) and *The Mind of the Old South* (1967). An early account of the Old South is found in James S. Buckingham's *The Slave States of America* (2 vols., 1842, reprinted 1974). The flavor of those days is tasted in *Travels in the Old South, 1783–1860, Selected from Periodicals of the Times* (2 vols., 1973) by Eugene L. Schwaab, Mrs. Roger A. Pryor's *Reminiscences of Peace and War* (1908, reprinted 1973) and *Memorials of a Southern Planter* (1890) by Susan D. Smedes which later appeared in a 1965 edition, edited by Fletcher M. Greene. Rosser H. Taylor's *Ante-Bellum South Carolina: A Social and Cultural History* (1942, reprinted 1970), Robert C. Reinders' chronicle of the Confederacy's greatest city *End of an Era: New Or-*

leans, 1850–1860 (1973) and *Hog Meat and Hoecake: Food Supply in the Old South, 1840–1860* (1972) by Sam B. Milliard shed further light on the people and customs.

Plantation life is described further in A. C. Land's *The Bases of Plantation Society* (1969); *Plantation Life Before Emancipation* (1892, reprinted 1973) by R. Q. Mallard; Morton Rubin's *Plantation County* (1951); *South Carolina Rice Plantation* (1945, reprinted 1973) by J. E. Easterby; and John W. Blassingame's *The Slave Community: Plantation Life in the Antebellum South* (1972). The relation between slavery and the general tenor of life here is traced by Leslie H. Owens in *This Species of Property: Slave Life and Culture in the Old South* (1975). Besides the great planters, the middle class and the slaves there was a fourth segment of society which is treated by Frank L. Owsley in *Plain Folk of the Old South* (1976).

There are two early contemporary accounts by Frederick L. Olmsted: *A Journey in the Back Country* (1860, reprinted 1970), and *A Journey in the Seaboard Slave States* (1856, reprinted 1974). See Broadus Mitchell's *Frederick Law Olmsted: A Critic of the Old South* (1924, reprinted 1968). One of the most influential writings of this period was Harriet Beecher Stowe's *Uncle Tom's Cabin, Or, Life Among the Lowly* (many editions, 1965 ed. edited by John A. Woods), supplemented by her documentary justification of her indictment of slavery in *A Key to Uncle Tom's Cabin* (1853, reprinted 1968). She, in turn, is the subject of Robert F. Wilson's *Crusader in Crinoline: The Life of Harriet Beecher Stowe* (1941, reprinted 1972).

The trade in slaves is the subject of James Pope-Hennessy's *Sins of the Fathers: A Study of the Atlantic Slave Trade* (1968) and the overall picture of this institution is found in Henry Sherman's *Slavery in the United States of America* (1860, reprinted 1974) and in Donald Robinson's *Slavery in the Structure of American Politics* (1971). The growth of the abolitionist movement is seen in Austin Willey's *History of the Antislavery Cause in State and Nation* (1886, reprinted 1973) ; *Death of Slavery: The United States, 1837–1865* (1969) by Elbert B. Smith and Jesse Macy's *The Anti-Slavery Crusade* (1919, revised ed., 1976). Kinley J. Brauer shows in *Cotton Versus Conscience* (1976) the conflict between profit and morals that not all in the South could reconcile. Howell Cobb, owner of more than one thousand slaves, attempted a justification in *A Scriptural Examination of the Institution of Slavery in the United States: With Its Objects and Purposes* (1856, reprinted 1972). Harvey Wish has written about another defender of slavery : *George Fitzhugh: Propagandist for the Old South* (1962).

Not all in the South justified slavery as seen in Carl N. Degler's *The Other South: Southern Dissenters in the 19th Century* (1975). George M. Weston argued in his *Progress of Slavery in the United States* (1857, reprinted 1969) that the decline and eventual abolition of slavery might actually have economic benefits to the South. Among the sympathizers of the slaves were the daughters of a Southern aristocrat, Sarah Moore (1792–1873) and Angelina Emily Grimke (1805–1899), who are the subjects of Gerda Lerner's *The Grimke Sisters from South Carolina: Pioneers for Women's Rights and Abolition* (1971). Also of interest in this connection is Levi Coffin's *Reminiscences of Levi Coffin, the Reputed President of the Underground Railroad* (1898, reprinted 1968).

By the same token not all in the North were abolitionists and in *Gentlemen of Property and Standing: Anti-Abolition Mobs in Jacksonian America* (1971) Leonard L. Richards describes this other side of the coin.

Martin R. Delany's *The Condition, Elevation, Emigration and Destiny of the Colored People of the United States* (1852, reprinted 1968) is the earliest classic work on American Black nationalism. A good biography of this remarkable man is *Making of an Afro-American: Martin Robinson Delany, 1812–1855* (1971) by Dorothy Sterling. Henry L. Tragle's *Southampton Slave Revolt of 1831: A Compilation of Source Material* (1971) gives insights into the key rebellion of Nat Turner, one consequence of which was the passage of stricter slave codes by nearly every Southern state. Arna Bontemps traces the life of an influential abolitionist and Black leader in *Free at Last: The Life of Frederick Douglass* (1972). From Douglass himself, we have *Narratives of the Life of Frederick Douglass* (1845, reprinted 1973). An escaped slave is the subject of Frances T. Humphreville's *Harriet Tubman: Flame of Freedom* (1967) and *Harriet Tubman: Conductor on the Underground Railway* (1955) by Ann Petry.

Many Southern writers influenced the thought and culture of the South. Some of the more important are recorded in the following: William P. Trent's *William Gilmore Simms* (1892, reprinted 1973); Jon L. Wakelyn's *The Politics of a Literary Man: William Gilmore Simms* (1973); *Henry Timrod: Laureate of the Con-*

federacy (1928, reprinted 1973) by Henry T. Thompson; *Henry Timrod* (1963) and *Sidney Lanier: The Man, the Poet, the Critic* (1968) by Edd W. Parks; Edwin Mim's *Sidney Lanier* (1905, reprinted 1968); *Augustus Baldwin Longstreet: A Study of the Development of Culture in the South* (1969) by John D. Wade; Rayburn S. Moore's *Paul Hamilton Hayne* (1973); *Richard Henry Wilde: His Life and Selected Poems* (1966) by Edward B. Tucker; Otis C. Skipper's *J.D.B. De Bow: Magazinist of the Old South* (1958) and Charles H. Bohner's *John Pendleton Kennedy: Gentleman from Kentucky* (1961). *Hinton Rowan Helper: Abolitionist-Racist* (1965) by Hugh C. Bailey is a good biography of the author of *Impending Crisis of the South*.

Religion has always been important in the shaping of the Southern ethos. *The Great Revival, 1787–1805: The Origins of the Southern Evangelical Mind* (1972) by John B. Boles is a good introduction to this subject. Other studies include Robert B. Semple's *The History of the Rise and Progress of the Baptists in Virginia* (1894, reprinted 1973); *The History of the Methodist Episcopal Church, South* (1894, reprinted 1972) by Alexander Gross; Jeremiah J. O'Connell's *Catholicity in the Carolinas and Georgia: Leaves of Its History* (1879, reprinted 1972); *They Came to Louisiana: Letters of a Catholic Mission, 1854–1882* (1970) edited by Sister Dorothea O. McCants; and *Presbyterians in the South: Volume 1, 1607–1861* (1963) by Ernest T. Thompson. As with so many ethical questions, slavery was to split some of the religious denominations in the South from their Northern counterparts. A contemporary justification for such division is given by Orange Scott in *Grounds for Secession from the*

Methodist Episcopal Church (1848, reprinted 1969).

The Life and Letters of James Henley Thornwell (1875, reprinted 1969) by Benjamin M. Palmer gives a good account of this leading Presbyterian educator. One Southerner was to affect education both North and South as described by James B. Conant in *Thomas Jefferson and the Development of American Public Education* (1962). *A Documentary History of Education in the South Before 1860* (5 vols., 1949–1953), edited by E. W. Knight, is a thorough survey. Higher education comes into focus in Ellis M. Coulter's *College Life in the Old South* (1974) and in Colyer Meriwether's *The History of Higher Education in South Carolina* (1889, reprinted 1972 and edited by Herbert B. Adams).

A sampling of men who had an impact on the Cotton Kingdom would include *Jefferson and Our Times: The Jeffersonian Heritage* (1973) by Dumas Malone; *Jefferson Davis* (1907, reprinted 1966) by William E. Dodd; *John C. Calhoun: American Portrait* (1950), a Pulitzer Prize winner by Margaret Coit; Henry S. Foote's *Casket of Reminiscences* (1874, reprinted 1974); *The Correspondence of Robert Toombs, Alexander H. Stephens and Howell Cobb* (1913, reprinted 1970) by Ulrich B. Phillips; William H. Russell's *My Diary North and South* (2 vols., 1862, reprinted 1974); J. W. Du Bose's *The Life and Times of William Lowndes Yancey* (2 vols., 1892, reprinted 1973); *The Cradle of the Confederacy: Or, the Times of Troup, Quitman and Yancey* (1876, reprinted 1975) by Joseph Hodgson; Mrs. Chapman Coleman's *The Life of John J. Crittenden* (2 vols., 1871, reprinted 1970); Allen Johnson's *Stephen A. Douglas: A Study in American Politics* (1908, reprinted 1970); *Stephen*

Douglas: The Last Years, 1857–1861 (1971) by Damon Wells; *Henry Clay and the Art of American Politics* (1957) by Clement Eaton and Phillip C. Auchampaugh's *James Buchanan and His Cabinet on the Eve of Secession* (1926, reprinted 1965).

The inevitability of secession did not suddenly arise but rather gradually evolved over the years. One of the first hints of the later, terrible events is depicted by William W. Freehling in *Prelude to Civil War: The Nullification Controversy in South Carolina, 1816–1836* (1968). Also of interest is *Democratic Politics and Sectionalism: The Wilmot Proviso Controversy* (1967) by Chaplain W. Morrison.

A good analysis of the movement towards secession is *The Course of the South to Secession* (1911, reprinted 1975) by Ulrich B. Phillips. Other worthwhile sources are P. M. Hamer's *The Secession Movement in South Carolina, 1847–1852* (1918, reprinted 1971); *The Secession Movement in Virginia, 1847–1861* (1934, reprinted 1970) by Henry T. Shanks and Percy L. Rainwater's *Mississippi: Storm Center of Secession, 1856–1861* (1938, reprinted 1969).

A largely unrecognized factor in the Cotton Kingdom is the theme of Fletcher Greene's *The Role of the Yankee in the Old South* (1972).

The noted historian, C. Vann Woodward, discusses the peculiar position of the South in *The Burden of Southern History* (rev. ed. 1968). An interesting biography of the author of *The Cotton Kingdom,* for which this bibliography has been prepared, is *Democrat and Diplomat: The Life of William H. Dodd* (1968) by Robert Dallek.

INDEX